Triumphs of Tenacity

(3

Triumphs of Tenacity

Yusra Mariyam

FIRST EDITION

978-1-80541-667-8 (paperback)

978-1-80541-666-1 (ebook)

Dedications

To my beloved children and husband.

Your unwavering support and encouragement have been my strength throughout these four years at university. This book is a testament to your love and belief in me.

Thank you for being my rock.

To all my teachers at Anglia Ruskin University.

My heartfelt gratitude goes to all the teachers in every module for their teaching and support, helping me to pass all the modules.

To my *amma* (mother), for giving birth to me and raising me with love and care.

To all my siblings, as we are all one blood imparted from our amma (mother) and *abba* (father), sharing the same journey, as one family, in upbringing, and for all the love that we still share amongst each other.

And finally, my abba, who was my greatest supporter from birth until his passing. Who cared for me, provided for me, and instilled in me the value of education, despite being illiterate himself. He taught me invaluable lessons and proverbs that strengthened my character, made me patient, and turned me into a fighter through every stage of life, regardless of the circumstances.

I would like to dedicate the following verses and prayers or my *abba*:

Quran, Chapter 17, Verse 24: 'My Lord, have mercy upon them as they brought me up [when I was] small.' Ameen.

'My Lord, forgive my *abba*, and grant him the highest rank in heaven.' Ameen.

Contents

Acknowledgements

I would like to express my deepest gratitude to Anglia Ruskin University for accepting my application and offering me the opportunity to pursue my undergraduate International Business Management degree between 2020-2024. Without this opportunity, I would not have graduated or considered myself as becoming educated, and I would not have developed the passion and inspiration to write this book.

This book is a detailed account of my personal stories, along with my four-year university journey, highlighting the challenges I faced, and the successes I accomplished. Documenting my work, including assignments and presentations, was not an easy task. It has been a great honour to have my editor, Alice Tindsley, by my side. Her meticulous attention to detail and encouragement pushed me to excel. Her guidance has been instrumental in shaping this book. Additionally, to complete this book, extensive research and numerous sources have been referenced. All the work has been paraphrased, and the ideas have been expressed in my own words and concepts.

To my university colleagues and friends, who provided endless support and encouragement. Your insights and suggestions were invaluable.

To everyone who read early drafts and provided feedback, thank you for your time and insights. Your contributions have played a crucial part in sharing my story.

Lastly, to my readers, for your interest and support. This book is for you.

Preface

In the journey of life, we often encounter obstacles that seem insurmountable.

Triumphs of Tenacity is my testament to the power of resilience, determination, and unwavering faith. Since arriving in the UK as a child, life has thrown many challenges my way. From educational setbacks to cultural adjustments, I battled each one and emerged stronger every time. At first, these mountains seemed impossible to climb, and I found myself giving in, choosing a life that did not align with my childhood dreams. But finally, I found the warrior within me and the drive to reclaim my dreams.

As a child, I had specific dreams for my future, hoping to embark on a career within the police force or practising law. I wanted to help others during their time of need or change lives in a role within the legal system. For reasons beyond my control, these dreams were crushed, forcing me to reconsider where my life would lead. Though my career ambitions fell by the wayside, I embraced a new life as a mother, harnessing my determination, and using it to help my children thrive. I threw myself into family life and adored motherhood, but deep down, I still dreamed of personal evolution and a career I could be proud of. Though my life was rich and full of love, the path I had envisaged for myself as a child became a distant memory.

As often as life throws hurdles at us, it also throws us opportunities, though these are often a lot harder to see and embrace. One such opportunity unexpectedly came my way, and despite self-doubt and the fear of failure, I recognised that I needed to reclaim the boldness and determination I had once had and jump at the chance. The offer of a university degree in international business appeared out of nowhere and, to my surprise, I seized it. My journey into education as a mature student held a myriad of barriers and difficult emotions, but it was also marked by self-growth and the rediscovery of my inner power. With the support of my family and led by the guiding light of my late *abba's* wisdom, I not only began learning the intricacies of the business world but discovered that I must somehow re-form a lost faith in myself if I were to succeed. My narrative highlights the importance of patience, self-belief, and the willingness to seek help. My experiences underscore the impact of compassionate teachers, and the transformative power of education. I recognised how finding the fighter within me was a much harder path than simply giving in and accepting failure, but I also learned the tools to travel that difficult road and cast aside the feelings of doubt that would hold me back.

Putting my journey into words has not been easy. However, owning my trials and emotional roller coaster has been rewarding. Looking back on the hardships, not only during my studies but also over the course of my life, has reinforced my understanding of the impact of education, as well as the importance of our will to evolve as individuals. A constant beacon of hope in my life has been my *abba* (father), and revisiting my time with him, his words of wisdom, and the day we lost him has been a painful yet valuable voyage. Though I have never let go of the wisdom he bestowed upon me throughout my life, I have seen how much this has moulded me as a person. The power of words and guidance should never be underestimated.

In this book, I have shared the knowledge I gained during my course, as well as the personal developments that came with it. I have conquered not only the practical elements of a degree in International Business, but also the intimate battles that could have halted my progress. Studying for a degree and empowering myself through education has inspired me to navigate life's challenges in a new light, and I hope this serves to inspire all who face their own battles.

My story is not just a recounting of struggles and triumphs, but a celebration of the human spirit's ability to overcome adversity. It is a reminder that with perseverance and faith, we can conquer the impossible and defy all odds.

Introduction

Yusra Mariyam's personal journey is a monument to the power of resilience, the importance of family support, the metamorphosis that comes with education, and the strength found in embracing one's heritage and faith.

At a young age, Yusra and her family relocated to the UK, where she was faced with the challenges of navigating a new world, finding her place within an unknown culture, and mastering a new language. Despite the many challenges faced by a young child suddenly entering an alien reality, Yusra discovered the determination and boldness of her spirit, successfully integrating into her new country and thriving. This boldness saw her develop a dream of serving the community as a police officer, fuelled by the desire to make a tangible difference in the lives of others and help people in their time of need. However, this noble dream was dashed by the height restrictions imposed by the British police force at the time. Faced with a barrier that had no solution, Yusra redirected her drive to support others, and turned her ambitions towards the field of law, hoping to effect change through the legal system.

When flaws in the education system left Yusra without the qualifications to pursue her career in law, she instead embraced a more traditional life as a mother and home-maker. Though fulfilled by family life, Yusra still hoped for a career and entered the world of work when her children were old enough.

Through chance, she was offered a role studying international business at Anglia Ruskin University and embarked on the unexpected resumption of her education as a mature student.

With this change of direction came new challenges, and Yusra had to reclaim the childhood strengths she had once found came so naturally. This book follows Yusra on her journey through adult education, combining the mountains she had to climb, the personal demons she had to face, and imparting the Business information she learned during her studies. With each chapter, Yusra shares the content of her course, and the challenges she met with each one, following her as she dug deep into herself and uncovered the self-assuredness and determination she had mastered as a child in a new country.

A seamless blend of the experience of studying International Business as a mature student and the self-discovery she was forced to undertake along the way, Yusra's story transcends her intimate challenges and touches on the broader themes of identity, belonging, and the pursuit of dreams, despite societal and personal setbacks. In her own words, Yusra combines the ins and outs of learning how to succeed in the world of business with the understanding of how to succeed in life itself, proving to be a beacon of hope for those following the same path.

Her memoir highlights the significance of finding solutions or alternatives when faced with closed doors and the sense of self that comes from embracing one's history, heritage, and faith. Yusra's journey is a powerful reminder that hardships and obstacles are not the end of the road, but rather opportunities to find new paths and grow from the challenge. Calling upon the wise words her father bestowed on her as a child, Yusra passes on this wisdom, allowing readers to also follow his guidance and embrace the words that served as a ray of hope, even in the darkest of times.

Through her story, Yusra offers practical lessons from her course in International Business, along with the emotional trials and tribulations that came with changing her life's direction. She proves that with determination and resilience, it is possible to take on any mountain and achieve one's dreams. In sharing her experience, Yusra hopes to inspire others to persevere in the face of adversity, embrace their heritage and faith, find strength in the support of their loved ones, and above all else, learn how to harness the power that lies within.

Chapter One:

Yusra

I, Yusra Mariyam, am an individual with a distinctly British mindset. I value directness and efficiency. I prefer cutting to the chase rather than engaging in circular discussions. I am the type of person who will, without fail, stand up every time life knocks me down. Which it has tried to do, many times.

During my teenage years, I aspired to become a police officer. The idea of being there when someone needs it the most, and to represent justice and safety, beckoned to me. I was convinced that it would be my calling, but this dream was thwarted by the height restrictions that the British police force had in place at the time. It felt unfair - the hopes I had for the career I longed for were snatched away from me by something so utterly beyond my control. In the 1990s, you had to be at least five foot and four inches tall to join the force, but I stopped growing just a few inches short of that, shattering the future I had dreamed of for so much of my childhood. After this, I rebuilt my dream with the idea of studying law, so that I might still be a symbol of hope for others, effecting change from within the legal system itself. I felt as though I had swept my disappointment under the rug and found a new path to follow after completing my

GCSEs and A-Levels. Yet, these aspirations also remained unfulfilled.

In the first three years of secondary education, I excelled in both maths and English, but when I entered my fourth year of schooling, everything changed. Mathematics became particularly challenging. During Year Four, our new mathematics teacher, who was also the head of our class, lacked the friendliness and supportiveness that many students needed to excel. She never revisited topics or provided clear examples for her pupils to follow. We tackled new concepts like ratios, proportions, complex fractions, and algebra without clear guidance, making these elements of the subject frustratingly inaccessible to me. I found it challenging to grasp these ideas and hesitated to seek help due to this teacher's strict and cold demeanour. The idea of raising my hand and drawing attention to my failings began to riddle me with anxiety whenever I felt that I needed guidance, so instead I struggled on alone, and inevitably, solved nothing. Unlike the upward trajectory I had experienced in my previous years in education, my performance in maths classes plummeted. Without proper explanations or examples, I found myself repeatedly heading in the wrong direction with classwork and struggling to tackle homework.

As the eldest sibling in my family, with illiterate parents, I had no one to turn to for support. I never plucked up the courage to ask for the help I needed, and when it came to sitting my GCSEs, I passed only two subjects – a crushing blow for a child with such big dreams. My determination saw me retake my GCSE exams the following year, studying even harder than before, yet remaining overwhelmingly out of my depth. Once again, I faced failure. This time, the reality of this disappointment weighed heavily on me. Despite my best efforts, I had only passed half of the tests needed to apply for the A-levels required to pursue a career in law. Leaving school with only two qualifications left my world spinning. Once again, I found myself with my dreams out of reach.

After experiencing the heartbreak of failing my exams twice, I felt lost, unsure of where to seek answers or guidance regarding my repeated failures. I felt powerless, left with no idea where to turn. I found myself wishing that I had experienced the good fortune to have a compassionate teacher. Maybe a teacher who smiled and understood their students' strengths and weaknesses could have been the crucial factor in my success during that pivotal stage of my life. Children need teachers with dedication and understanding in order to succeed, and this missing link led me twice to feelings of failure and defeat. Despite the challenges I knew I would face, I made the difficult decision to leave my education behind, giving up the idea of trying again and replacing it with a hunt for work of any kind. Something in me, however, never gave up hope that one day there might be hidden opportunities waiting for me on an alternative path.

I cherished my family's ancient wisdom, spanning far beyond my Bangladeshi roots, and passed down through generations. My faith remained steadfast, guiding me through life's challenges. My father, my *abba*, as we called him in our Bengali mother tongue, was a strong yet gentle figure who introduced me to important values, standing by my side and always silently supporting me. His experienced hands held mine during moments of uncertainty. He shared stories of resilience, recited wise proverbs, and taught me forgiveness. Despite his inability to assist me with academic subjects—his illiteracy and limited English forming a barrier between him and the help I needed—he consistently provided encouragement and instilled in me the importance of self-worth and self-education. He knew how much a good education would benefit me in the future and sought everything within his abilities to assist my siblings and I with this. His encouragement fuelled my ambition to reach high places, and he stressed the importance of reading the Quran, its insightful verses guiding me in times of doubt.

Despite my best efforts to overcome my academic challenges and pursue A-Levels with a view to study law, I had failed. Though I didn't feel that I myself was a failure, I knew that academic failure was not an easy obstacle to counter. However, my abba's unwavering motivation taught me to explore alternative paths, finding a new path when one route doesn't yield results.

"Have patience," he would tell us. "Hardship doesn't stay forever. The door never stays shut, and if you keep searching for the way to open it, you will see the light on the other side." Patience and persistence became my allies. His legacy remains my wellspring of strength, propelling me onward as I carry it forward.

Abba came to the UK in 1963 in search of better job opportunities, landing work as a labourer in a textile factory and supporting his elderly father and his younger siblings back in Bangladesh. He and my mother, my *amma* in Bengali, married in September 1969, and I was born five years later. We did not have any option but to remain apart, a family split between two different continents. Abba's job in the UK allowed him to support us, and no matter how hard the work was, he never once complained. He would visit us every chance he got, though sometimes we would have to wait more than a year to be reunited. With each visit I got older and bigger, but nothing had changed between us. He would stay for several months each time, taking me on outings to funfairs, or shopping for fruit from the market, spending every spare moment with me somewhere close by.

Though extremely intelligent, he was illiterate, having been denied access to education as a child in Bangladesh. Back then, education in Bangladesh was not free, and my *dada* (grandfather) could not afford the fees needed to send his sons to school. Instead, abba and his brothers worked on the family farm, grafting throughout their childhoods just to survive. This kind of near-poverty was not unusual in Bangladesh at the time, and abba's journey from the countryside's beating sun and fertile soil to raising his family in the UK was not an easy one. Before he had even met my amma, he had worked hard to successfully acquire British citizenship, and the UK was very much his home. As such, his children automatically became British citizens too, opening us up for futures he had never dreamed of as a child.

In contrast to this, my amma was lucky enough to complete her education up to the equivalent of year five in the UK, which, though low by today's standards, was an achievement in Bangladesh when she was a child. Her education, however, ended there, and was not nearly advanced enough to be considered literate. Like most traditional Muslim mothers when I was young, she was a homemaker, attentively raising our large family whilst my abba shed blood, sweat and tears as the breadwinner, determined that, unlike in his childhood, we would never see a day without food on the table.

When it was my turn to follow abba and make the almost five-thousand-mile journey to settle in the UK, the shift was stark, and quite frankly, terrifying. The first thing that hit me was the bitter cold. Winter was fiercely gripping the UK in November 1981, biting at my cheeks as I exited Heathrow Airport and stepped into my new life. The temperatures that year were well below zero degrees, at times hitting some of the lowest ever recorded in the country. And this was when my seven-year-old-self saw snow for the first time. Knee-deep and covering everything. Of course, I had heard of snow, but I had not imagined just how *cold* it would be or even realised that it was wet. This unexpected discovery made my new home feel even more alien to me, and at times I even briefly found myself longing for my old life back. I distinctly remember complaining to abba about the cold, the sudden shock to my senses dampening my enthusiasm for this new chapter of my life. As always, his words soothed me: "Don't worry my dear, you'll get used to it gradually." He was right, of course, and I learned to embrace the changes that surrounded me.

My name, Yusra, is of Arabic origin, meaning "ease" or "prosperity." The roots of this name are mentioned in the Quran, where it appears in the 94th chapter, specifically in Verse Six, along with the line, *"Verily with hardship comes ease."* As a child, I did not fully understand the power of this name, but now, in hindsight, I feel that my parents made the right choice. Even as a newborn baby, unaware of the world around me or the hardships that lay ahead, my abba saw something in me, naming me the very definition of strength and resilience.

Upon our arrival in the UK, like the rest of my family, I could only speak Bengali. The English language sounded fast and harsh in my ears, the strange sounds and words flowing around me without revealing their secrets. In Bangladesh, I had only completed the equivalent of Year One by UK standards, so my sudden introduction to the British education system was horrifically intimidating. I felt painfully small and out of my league.

Initially, I spent almost a year in a language unit learning English. Although it was strange and challenging at first, I gradually improved my understanding of English, learned syllables, and adapted to the language's rhythm and intonations. Within three to four months, without even realising the speed of my improvements, I felt confident conversing with teachers and peers.

In the language unit, we also received swimming lessons—which I was overjoyed to discover. As I stood in my bathing suit at the side of the pool during my first swimming lesson, I was bemused to have a lifeguard fitting swimming aids to my arms and around my stomach. Like most children, I had learned to swim from around the age of five in Bangladesh, paddling in nearby rivers and splashing at local swimming pools, but the precautions and safety measures being taken by the teachers made me nervous. As gingerly as I had first entered the country, I entered the pool. The unfamiliar environment made me wonder if I would be able to swim, as though somehow, I had been stripped of my swimming skills upon slipping into the water, washing away part of my identity. However, when I let go of the handrail, I realised that the pool was much shallower than I had expected, and I could stand on the bottom with ease. I had faced much deeper waters than these. Without a word, I removed my swimming aids—one by one—from my arms and then my waist. I hardly noticed the teachers brace themselves, ready to rescue me if I struggled, but within seconds, I was confidently testing the waters and revisiting my skills. I splashed and swam with delight, feeling so at home as the water embraced me, reclaiming the hobby I had enjoyed so much in Bangladesh. When I was finished, the teachers were full of questions, in awe that I could already swim so fluently and with such ease, despite my age. It seemed that they couldn't fathom how a shy girl who had not long arrived from Bangladesh and could barely speak a word of English could also possess so much skill and confidence in the water. They had underestimated me.

As swimming lessons continued, my teachers started testing me, challenging me to do more. They asked me to attempt diving from the high board, towering so tall over my seven-year-old self. This was something I had never done before, but I wasn't afraid. Without hesitation, I scaled the ladder that led to the diving board, taking a deep breath as I stood on the end. I glanced down at the water-filled pool, excitement and determination overpowering the nerves I felt. I let the nervousness drown, stretching out my arms and leaping into the air, feeling a rush as I plunged into the water. I resurfaced with a sense of accomplishment, realising that I had both reclaimed an old love as well as discovered something new to love.

The teachers approached me with further tests—swimming lengths, collecting items from the floor of the pool, and holding my breath underwater, even managing two minutes submerged without feeling an ounce of fear. Eventually, I was awarded a certificate recognising my advanced swimming skills. This felt like my first big achievement on British soil, soaring to the top of my swimming class, accompanied by another Bangladeshi girl. We were not two insignificant immigrant children, but a pair of high achievers with a passion. It was the confidence boost I needed, realising that I was not out of my depth or treading water in this strange country, but a vessel of potential, full to the brim. I turned my sights on mastering the English language next, and began thriving in the new world of education, with my head held high.

By July 1982, I had completed my time in the language unit and was proficient in English. When the summer was over and September arrived, I would join my peers in a mainstream primary school, entering Year Four. Over the following three years—the final years of primary school—we had classes in English, mathematics, science, and P.E.—which included my beloved swimming lessons. I struggled with science but found myself excelling in mathematics and English, thoroughly enjoying the subjects. P.E., however, was my favourite lesson of the week. I loved cross- country running, relishing the feeling of my heart pounding in my chest and the air flowing through my hair. I was chosen to represent my school in long jump competitions against other primary schools and proved myself worthy, coming in third place. I was appreciative of my British education and my time in school, understanding the opportunities that it was unlocking for me. Likewise, I sensed that my peers and teachers were appreciative of me, glad to have me in their midst as a friend, as well as representing the school in sporting competitions. I had the sense of truly belonging.

I had never watched television or seen a movie before moving to the UK, but all of a sudden, I had access to something that broadened my horizons incalculably and let my imagination soar. During my teenage years, I immersed myself in television shows like *"Dallas," "Dynasty," "The A-Team," "Knight Rider," "Superman," "Rambo,"* and *"The Incredible Hulk."* These action-packed adventures resonated with my nonconforming personality and joined my love of sports and physical activity, driving my inspiration for a career in the police force, unaware, at the time, that I would never be able to achieve that goal. Yet, in quiet moments, when tradition and modernity converged, I discovered my inner strength—an embodiment of both my *abba's* wisdom and my unique identity. My life wove together love, sacrifice, and tradition, placing myself at the crossroads of past and present, connecting generations.

Abba, with his unconventional perspective, didn't see me solely as a daughter, but also like a son. This outlook ignited my determination to uphold his principles. I embraced my role as a responsible daughter, my tomboyish spirit somehow seamlessly aligning with the legacy I unbegrudgingly felt responsible for. I can fondly recall, back in 1982, a few months after my arrival in the UK, abba took me out walking, and as we passed various shops, we came across a fruit and vegetable store. Abba stopped next to it, admiring the apples and grapes and other brightly coloured fruits on display. He then shared a story that I would cherish forever. He told me of his time in the UK, long before the rest of our family came to join him, when he was alone and missing us greatly. Despite his fondness for fruits, he refrained from purchasing them. Why? Because every time he touched an apple or tasted a grape, he thought of me—his daughter back in Bangladesh—who wouldn't have access to such fruits. Instead, he would put them back on the shelf, preferring to go without them than to relish them without me. However, now that I was with him, holding his hand, he joyfully declared, "We'll buy all of these fruits, and as father and daughter, we'll enjoy them together." He bought us a feast, and we sat together, eating every last piece. I can recall the way his eyes twinkled as we both bit into our first apple together, feeling love radiating from him, as sweet as the fruit itself.

We would often walk, abba and I, wandering the nearby shops and offices that made mazes for us to explore. As we would walk, hand in hand, he would gently impart his wisdom and share ancient proverbs. Our bond was incredibly close. He was my idol and my best friend. His lack of formal education was no reflection of his intelligence, but he struggled to pick up the English language, so I became his translator. It was a role I felt honoured to carry out, giving me the opportunity to guide him, just like he had guided me.

Growing into adulthood in an Asian and Muslim context during the 1990s and finding myself without the qualifications needed for higher education, I chose to instead follow the cultural norm, where women often married at a young age. At the age of twenty, I wholeheartedly embraced this commitment without hesitation or regret. The responsibilities of being a wife weighed on me, yet I faced them with resolute determination. My new path in life, however, took me away from my abba. I moved with my husband to London, five hours away from the small town I had grown up in, and the streets where I had once wandered hand-in-hand with my dad. We saw each other less and less as my family grew. The responsibilities of motherhood also grew, until my focus was almost entirely on raising my children and helping them thrive. My younger siblings each taking their turn to be my parent's companion and translator until we had all left home to follow our different paths. Abba never once held us back or asked us to stay. He understood the need to let us make our own journeys through life.

I became a mother to six children, each possessing distinct and beautiful personalities. Their laughter infused our home with warmth and vitality - a place of joy and love. Amidst their growth, I forgot my own aspirations. My dreams of becoming a become a police officer or a lawyer were replaced by a promise to help them achieve their own dreams, holding their hands through life's highs and lows, as abba had once held mine. My aspirations shifted entirely to being the best parent I could be, encouraging growth and education, aiming to open doors to their professional successes with the highest level of learning. Drawing from my own struggles, and the pain I had experienced when I couldn't pass my GCSEs, I made it my mission to support my children during their academic challenges. Where I couldn't provide assistance, I sought out tutors and assistance to ensure their success. My love for them fuelled a determination to protect them from the same failures in the educational system that I had faced, and the heartache I had suffered as a result.

After dedicating decades to being a full-time mother, and managing a thriving household, I made a life-changing decision. In 2017, when my youngest child was old enough, I decided to seek fulfilment beyond the domestic domain and enter the world of work. I was forty-three years old, and though I had never had a job before, this was not something I had ever been ashamed of. Being a homemaker and a mother *is* a full-time job. Especially when you are outnumbered six to one. I had adored having the privilege of seeing my family grow bigger and my kids grow taller, so it never truly felt like work, but it was also gruelling, exhausting, and stressful, and overflowing with love. They were my pride and joy, but now they were spreading their wings and starting new stages of their lives, so it was time I started mine. I knew I would find it difficult to even find work, given that my CV had very little to show, but I somehow managed to land myself an interview at an international business that provided leading services in customer management and business process outsourcing. Though my CV was barely a scrap of paper, the interviewers saw my potential, and before I knew it, I was sitting in the chair at my first real job, terrified but willing to try.

My new journey led me to a role in sales, where I flourished. I engaged with Business-to-Business (B2B) customers, skilfully building relationships through rapport. I conducted thorough financial business account reviews and actively promoted products and services. I had no idea that my responsibilities would come so naturally to me, and I felt that I was starting to thrive there. In this chapter of my life, I blended my innate capacities for organisation, dealing with people and setting goals with a business acumen that I never knew I possessed, proving to those around me that determination and adaptability are timeless qualities.

But in just two years, this adventure was over. The challenges posed by the COVID-19 pandemic, saw my job in jeopardy, with the likelihood of this job coming to an end, after three months of furlough, looking incredibly high.

I found myself once more searching for career opportunities, hoping that my limited experience in a professional setting would not be my downfall. In May 2020, I stumbled across an advertisement by a recruitment agency in London that stated, "*Learn and Earn.*" I booked an appointment and travelled to see an agent, driven by the possibility of a new venture into business. As soon as I entered the office, this agent greeted me with a question I never thought I would answer: "Do you want to apply for a degree?"

I was taken aback. The question hung in the air, leaving me momentarily speechless. I had come seeking employment, not academic pursuits. The 'learn' part on the advertisement seemed to be something for other people, not for me. A degree was something that had never crossed my mind.

Summoning my voice, I managed a response. "Are you serious?" I mustered. "I came here to look for a job. There's no chance of me pursuing a degree!" My disbelief echoed through the room. *How could I even consider a university degree when my educational achievements consisted of just two GCSEs? They were either making fun of me or wasting my time.* These scattered thoughts swirled wildly around my brain, lacking order or continuity, all disconnected. My high school maths teacher sprang to mind, her stern face once again criticizing my efforts. I saw once more my GCSE results letter, with failure marked in black and white, resurfacing from distant memories to taunt me.

The agent persisted, armed with information from my CV, reassuring me of my capabilities. Then it was my abba's face that came dancing into my racing mind, with his soft smile and his strong words.

I revealed my experience in sales, engaging with B2B customers, and promoting business products and services. With this, the agency proposed the programme, "International Business Management with Foundation Year." They started coaxing more details from me, encouraging me that this pathway would allow me to build a solid footing, bridging the gap between my existing knowledge and the requirements of a fully-fledged degree. The gap between undereducated to graduate.

So, I stood at this crossroads, pondering the implausible - a journey from sales to academia. Perhaps in this unexpected twist lay the possibility of conquering what I had always thought was impossible. I was prompted to take a seat. As I studied the course details, a realisation washed over me—the striking parallels between my previous employment responsibilities and the versatile aspects of business management. My previous role encompassed sales, marketing, advertising, business enhancement strategies, product promotion, effective communication, stakeholder satisfaction, and revenue generation. These elements, I realised, embodied the essence of business management, both at a national and international level. I had always pictured myself as a minor player in a company, carrying out basic duties and striving for nothing more, knowing that anything else was out of my reach. Patiently, the agency staff guided me through the necessary steps, urging me to write a personal statement and complete the application forms. Despite enduring anxiety and a whirlwind of emotions, the support from the agency saw me transform from a hesitant self-doubter to someone eager to seize the opportunity before me.

The monumental click of the submission button brought a brief sense of relief, echoed in the agent's proud facial expression. However, my own expression, no doubt, revealed a different story, with tensions engraved across my face from every angle - a mixture of self-doubt and perplexion about the episode that had just unfolded. Despite my inner turmoil, the agent stepped in, offering reassurance that my decision to apply for the degree was indeed the start of something big. The journey home, though, saw my self-doubt double. *Why had I got so carried away? Why did I not simply apply for a job? Why did I imagine this road could be for me?* I was, once again, chasing the impossible.

I spent the next two days dwelling on my foolishness, a penetrating feeling of emptiness that refused to go away. I was not naive - I recognised my own limitations. My previous academic failings proved them, which was why finding an email from Anglia Ruskin University sitting smugly in my inbox that Monday morning changed everything. To my astonishment, the email contained an invitation: a telephone interview for a place on an undergraduate degree course, scheduled for the upcoming Friday. I had just four days to prepare myself, but this was new territory for me, and I had no idea where to begin. Despite the previous frustration that I felt about wasting my time there, I promptly reached out to the agency for guidance. That glimmer of hope had returned.

I was advised that being well-informed on current affairs, especially Brexit and COVID-19, could benefit me during the interview process. I had never been particularly interested in following the news, yet suddenly the focus of my entire week swerved to becoming well-informed about these topics. As I diligently trawled through Google results and news articles, preparing for the impending interview with Anglia Ruskin University, I was hit by a sudden realisation—I wanted this. In fact, I *really* wanted this.

On the much-anticipated Friday, at precisely 4:30 p.m., an interviewer from the university called. To my surprise and frustration, the questions weren't related to the topics I had so meticulously researched. Instead, they probed my general knowledge, testing my IQ and logic. From defining globalisation to explaining international business management, the questions challenged me. I was then asked why I believed I was well-suited to pursue this degree. I found myself hesitating, gripped by imposter syndrome. Yet, a flicker of determination still glimmered within me. In that pivotal moment, I recalled the art of job interview skills.

Even if precise answers eluded me, I resolved to respond positively. I started to believe. "I'm eager to grow and prepared to learn," I assured the interviewer. This mindset shift eventually became my secret weapon—a masterstroke that transformed uncertainty into possibility.

During the interview, I confidently answered five of the ten questions. However, the remaining five posed more of a challenge. The interviewer didn't see this as a weakness. They saw my potential, determination, and willingness to strive and achieve. Finally, the gruelling interview concluded, and relief washed through my veins. Yet, this relief was tainted by shame, which clung to me like shadows in a dimly lit room. Doubt gnawed at my confidence - after all, I had stumbled through my GCSEs, I had seen my dreams slip through my fingers like sand. How could I dare to dream of even pursuing a university degree, let alone completing one?

After another tumultuous weekend, Monday brought one of the most significant moments of my life: an acceptance email from Anglia Ruskin University. Starting in September 2020, I would begin studying for an undergraduate degree in International Business Management with a Foundation Year. An actual university considered me suitable for an undergraduate degree. My family shared in this unexpected joy, their pride on my behalf echoing the pride I had felt on behalf of each of my children as they achieved their dreams. Now, aged forty-six, it was finally *my* turn.

The following months were a rollercoaster. The persistent feeling of anticipation clashed with the intensity of my imposter syndrome. As I prepared for the degree, that haunting question still loomed: Could I navigate the program successfully? Yet, I reminded myself that I had four months before beginning the degree—a window of time to address and alleviate those fears. I had to keep reminding myself of the encouragement my *abba* had unwaveringly given to me, even when it seemed I had failed, and the faith he had always had in the strength of my soul. Between May and mid-September 2020, my life resembled a tapestry woven with threads of joy and fear. The world grappled with the pandemic, burdened by COVID-19 cases and great loss. Yet, within this global struggle, I carried my own unique, internal battle.

Stepping outside during those four months with the limited allowance of the COVID-19 restrictions, the promise of a new adventure beckoned. The sun bathed my surroundings in warmth, and the open summer field embraced me. The sky stretched out, a brilliant blue canvas, while birds orchestrated a symphony of their own. I would savour these moments of freedom, my heart swelling with excitement, knowing that university lay on the horizon, and I was heading straight towards it. I fought the looming shadow of doubt clinging to my thoughts like a persistent rain cloud. My new-found resilience fighting those intrusive thoughts, countering them with answers.

How would my online university unfold? With a new experience every day.

How could I successfully navigate this new digital-learning ecosystem? With my willingness to embrace new challenges.

Am I actually doing this? Without a doubt, yes, I am!

These questions assailed my mind, heart, and soul, but this time, I knew the answers.

As it turned out, a call from my manager lit up my phone around this time with the unexpected news that although the troubles of COVID-19 had indeed seen my position at the company close, they wanted to offer me an alternative role and keep me on as an employee. Although this was fantastic news, and the job security was a huge relief, it also meant that I would be taking on this new position within the company and learning the ropes of my new role at the same time as starting my degree. It was a daunting idea, and I was concerned that the dual commitments would stretch me too thin and have an impact on my performance in both areas, yet I knew it was something I had to do. It was heartening, knowing that the company valued me as a member of the team enough to accommodate me in a new position, and had faith in my abilities. It seemed suddenly apparent that both my employers and the educators at the university had more faith in me than I had in myself. Though it would be a challenge, it was also a necessity.

Finally, September arrived, marking the grand entrance into my academic journey. The sapphire sky above seemed to cheer me on. The birds' song rang with encouragement. The summer of 2020 was one of uncertainty for everyone, but as it drew to a close, my uncertainty faded. Yes, those niggling fears and reminders of failure remained, but the academic landscape beckoned, and a new path through life began.

My journey began with a childhood laced with uncertainty but supported by my abba's unwavering belief in me. My sudden introduction to a new country left me with the need to adapt quickly, forging the ability to embrace huge changes and develop resilience. My dad's guidance was a constant source of motivation, pushing me to explore new paths, and encouraging me to persevere. He was never doubting or disappointed in me, even after failing my GCSEs twice.

I spent decades as a mother and a homemaker, finally entering the world of work aged forty-three as timidly as I first entered the country or had first entered the swimming pool all those years ago. When I joined the workforce, I knew that I could draw on my past to find my strength. I could search inside myself for the determined young swimmer and recall the wise words of my *abba* from our many walks together. I took these experiences and took the plunge.

My new ventures did not come without obstacles, having to learn an entirely new skillset rapidly and think on my feet, but the determination to succeed was still there.

My experience in sales had developed a basic understanding of the way a business looks from the inside and taught me about revenue generation and business enhancement strategies. But it had also honed my people skills, showed me that I was a fast learner, and gave me a new perception of my value in the workplace. I realised that, as my business degree lay in my future, I would not only need to draw from my past but also look at my present and recognise the trade skills I already possessed. My past and my present were the tools I needed for my success in the future. I knew that my apprehensions were unfounded and that I indeed had more life experience and worth than I believed, but anxiety and self-doubt would be my biggest hurdles to overcome. Balancing my responsibilities as a mother, full-time worker, and my upcoming studies would not be easy, but I did not know that this would teach me the true meaning of resilience, determination, and willpower, nor that these traits were already lying within me. They lay in the very meaning of my name.

I am sharing my story as a reminder that tough times can lead to great achievements. Despite our setbacks, we can rise, like a phoenix from the ashes, again and again. Just like my abba had, we can overcome hardships, shape our futures, and maybe even inspire others to do the same. We all possess the inner strength to overcome significant challenges. We can move forward, fuelled by tenacity.

Chapter Two:

Foundation Year

In mid-September 2020, as the world struggled with the ongoing pandemic and the COVID-19 cases continued to rise, there was a looming possibility of another lockdown in the UK. It was undeniably a challenging time for many, with news of suffering and loss echoing worldwide. Television screens constantly highlighted efforts to combat the virus, seeking solutions to halt its spread. Across countries, including the UK, intensive work focused on vaccine implementation, approval, and public distribution. The goal was to rescue people, instil a sense of security, and restore normalcy to daily life. During this time of uncertainty and talks of "the new normal", I embarked on my journey towards my own, personal "new normal"—my attempt to leave behind my past perceived failure and obtain my International Business Management degree.

Semester 1

During the pandemic, Zoom had swiftly become the go-to method for virtual communication since the country had first entered lockdown. The platform's sudden rise to becoming a household name saw me heading for online classes via Zoom, introducing me to a brand-new style of learning. Despite my basic technology skills, I navigated the new platform by following step-by-step procedures and timidly clicking on links. I must admit that initially, this presented an alien experience, but refusing to fall at the first hurdle motivated me to improve my technological proficiency, knowing that developing these skills unaided would be imperative to my success. Although it was challenging at first, I eventually mastered Zoom's virtual platform, making attending classes a weekly routine. To many, this may seem like a small achievement, but for someone who had previously had a tendency to let gnawing self-doubt halt personal progress, this first step alone taught me two valuable things: How much I desired to succeed, and how willing I was to do so. This first step allowed me to attend my online classes, interact with various tutors for different modules, and connect with my classmates.

In my foundation year, I tackled several modules during the first semester. These included 'Research Skills 1,' and 'Personal Development in Professional Settings,' both of which were conducted as online classes on Saturdays. Additionally, I engaged in 'Professional Communications' on Tuesday evenings at 6 p.m., and 'Data Skills' on Thursday evenings at the same time. This online approach to pursuing my degree peppered my existing dual responsibilities: full-time work and being a mother to six children. Weekday evenings and Saturdays became the only feasible days for me to complete my studies and work on assignments, but

I quickly adjusted to this new regimen, enthused by absorbing the information I was being gifted with in each class. I delved into module topics with eagerness. While these subjects were accessible to me, they still posed challenges - the focus of the assignments for these modules was essay writing.

Despite doing well in English during my first few years of high school, I had never completed assignments that required Harvard-style referencing. This new method presented a learning curve for me, initially feeling significantly behind classmates who already had experience with higher education. Additionally, after decades away from academic study, adjusting to writing essays that aligned with the assignment brief was a tough task. Nevertheless, with the support of my tutors at Anglia Ruskin University, I persisted. I recognised that adherence to these requirements was essential for passing the modules.

My new tutors stood in stark contrast to the formidable teachers I had encountered during my GCSEs, and the sudden realisation that I wasn't entirely alone and could access support when I needed it gave me a whole new outlook on education. I suddenly understood that it could take one bad teacher to send a student into a downward spiral, but it could take one good teacher to rectify this. My assisted exploration of Harvard-style referencing was fascinating. As something I had not previously known existed, this new system provided structure that I realised aligned with my learning style. As I probed deeper into each module text-book, I gained a clearer understanding of what this referencing style entailed, and how it should be meticulously incorporated into my assignments, opening me up to my first module: 'Research Skills 1.'

Research Skills 1

In 'Research Skills 1,' I encountered an intriguing topic: the 'Marshmallow Test.' This psychological experiment involved children aged four. The foundational information for this test was sourced from the scholarly book *Pursuing Human Strengths*, authored by Martin Bolt and Dana S. Dunn, in its second edition, published in 2016. The 'Marshmallow Test' aimed to assess the self-control and self-efficacy of these young participants. During the test, children faced a tempting choice: they could have an immediate sweet treat, or if they waited patiently, they would receive a double reward. The longer they resisted the immediate gratification, the more treats they could ultimately enjoy. This experiment shed light on the diverse abilities of children to delay gratification and exercise self-control. Personally, I found this topic profound and meaningful, as it reminded me of abba's teachings: "Patience leads to better results." Indeed, patience and self-control are crucial for achieving superior outcomes, a lesson that resonates both with my abba's wisdom and the insights from the 'Marshmallow Test' (Bolt & Dunn, 2016).

The module's final assignment was centred around investigating how digital technology can improve professionals' experiences in the workplace and within organisations. This topic resonated with me, as it highlighted my own technological limitations. When faced with technology-based challenges at work, I tended to panic, relying on my basic skills and embarrassingly requiring support from managers and colleagues to resolve any issues. I was well aware of the benefits of computer literacy and familiarity with software relating to the day-to-day running of an organisation, but until this point, I had not felt particularly driven to achieve this. I became aware that if I aspired to apply for better and higher positions, I needed to learn and master advanced technological tools.

The required textbook for our class research and assignment in this module was *The New Digital Workplace: How New Technologies Revolutionise Work.* It was authored by Kendra Briken, Shiona Chillas, Martin Krzywdzinski, and Abigail Marks in 2020. The book provides a rigorous examination of how digital technologies impact work and organisations. This reminded me of an experience from early 2019 when I applied for a Junior Account Manager role at my current company. During the final interview round, I was required to create a presentation demonstrating how I could be an effective Account Manager. Although I struggled initially, I did extensive research online to try and produce the presentation slides. Despite my efforts, other candidates vying for the same position delivered top-notch presentations that aligned better with the role's expectations, ultimately securing the position. This had been a hard blow for me, feeling that I was at a disadvantage, trying to keep up with my colleagues. Although we had equal experience and equal skills, I was not their equal when it came to digital abilities, and it showed. This underscores the importance for professionals to continually advance their skills and stay abreast of technology in order to thrive in the workplace and contribute effectively within organisations.

Despite this, I had still not managed to catch up with the computer skills that came naturally to others. For most people, using computers had become the daily norm, but at the time I entered the workforce, I had barely needed to use them, focusing instead on motherhood.

Although advancing my knowledge in technology and reflecting on the 'Marshmallow Test' imparted profound lessons, it was the 'Marshmallow Test' that instilled in me resilience and effective coping strategies to overcome disappointments and critical challenges. I realised that I was engaging in my own 'Marshmallow Test' - the more self-control and perseverance I displayed during my studies, the more it would ultimately lead to a greater reward - my degree.

Personal Development in Professional Settings

I took the assignment for the 'Personal Development in Professional Settings' module to heart, with the realisation that what I learned during these classes would not stay in a professional setting, but spill into my personal life, too. The module involved several key tasks. First, I assessed my current skill set, pinpointing areas with growth potential. Next, I outlined my employment experiences and honed in on my career objectives. Following that, I identified my strengths and weaknesses, emphasising skills relevant to advancing towards my career goals. Lastly, I devised strategies for professional growth. I realised that for anyone wanting to succeed, whether it be in education, a career, or in their personal lives, these skills are the key to growth. I emphasise this because you, simply as a human being, will find that these four steps will assist your evolution: assess, outline, identify, strategize.

For me, as far as the development of my skills within a professional setting, I identified that the areas in which I needed the most growth were my technological skills, enhancing communication, and expanding my network via platforms such as LinkedIn. In this particular module, I received a lot of support in my understanding from two key textbooks: *Skills for Success* and *The Graduate Career Guidebook*.

Professional Communications

The 'Professional Communications' module was the third module in the foundation year's first semester. The assignment aimed to explore how Anglia Ruskin University (ARU) could enhance students' employability skills, while working within a limited budget. The focus areas included foreign language classes, personal communication, information and communication technology (ICT) skills, and critical digital literacy. Among these, digital literacy was identified as the ideal employability skill, and students were encouraged to achieve a superior level of technological proficiency. To complete this module assignment, students reinforced their language skills by participating in the 'Digital Literacy Project' journal and referring to an article in *The Guardian* newspaper on language skills. Overall, the 'Professional Communications' and 'Personal Development in Professional Settings' modules were both literacy-based. The assignments involved conducting investigations in journals, articles, and textbooks. Fortunately, I found these two modules straightforward and didn't encounter any significant challenges, for which I was grateful. I came to realise that a large part of this success came down to a previous skill I had never even realised I possessed - the ability to communicate.

Having grown up with parents who spoke very little English between them, the communications of my early years were always in Bengali. When I heard my abba's philosophical insight and my amma's loving words, it was always in their mother tongue - my first language. As my English skills developed, I became their personal translator. It would be my responsibility to attend doctor's appointments, council meetings, and the solicitor's office, conveying to my parents the information that was right there in front of them, yet inaccessible. I was confident in speaking to anyone, and comfortable in settings that other children may have found strange or intimidating. I was aware of the importance of clarity and detail, as well as the value of communication. I was entirely oblivious at the time that this experience was something that would be of great value in my future, and I had remained in this oblivion up until I began studying the 'Business Communications' module.

Combining my ability to clearly communicate important information, my understanding of multi- lingual and international communication, and developing my digital communication skills felt natural, and I realised that this would be one of my great strengths in an international business setting.

Data Skills

During my first semester, I the most significant challenge I encountered was in the 'Data Skills' module. This module primarily focused on mathematical concepts such as percentages, ratios, and problem-solving strategies. I had already identified, during my 'Personal Development in a Professional Setting' module, that although my digital skills were lacking, my weakest area lay in mathematics, and this struggle became increasingly evident during the course. Throughout the initial four weeks of online sessions for 'Data Skills,' I grappled with understanding even the basics of addition, subtraction, multiplication, and division. Other mathematical topics felt like complex puzzles, despite my efforts to explore and engage in class discussions. The root cause of this struggle was my lapse in recalling essential mathematical rules related to percentages, mean, mode, median, ratios, and long-form problem-solving strategies. My high school math teacher's face loomed in the back of my mind, and I began, for the first time during my studies, to dread logging into my online classes.

During online sessions, I appeared withdrawn and silent, unable to actively participate in class discussions, where most students were engaged. The bitter sting of my multiple GCSE failures reared its ugly head once more. I realised that I had spent years sweeping these topics under the mat, avoiding complex mathematical challenges anywhere possible throughout my whole adult life.

Fortunately, the data skills tutor noticed my struggle and reached out to offer support. The tutor inquired whether I required additional assistance or one-on-one guidance. Despite my emotional struggle, I managed to hold back my tears in front of my classmates. Though I had also identified my digital skills as a hurdle, my mathematical weakness felt much more personal. I tactfully suggested to my tutor that my son, who was at the time studying A-level mathematics, could be my initial source of support. If my son's assistance would not suffice, I would seek help from the tutor directly. In reality, the idea of reaching out to the tutor and fully revealing my shameful shortcoming churned my stomach. Despite the tutor's warmth, I could not help but draw the link to the teacher who had made me feel so foolish during my school years. Looking for help outside of my own family was not something I felt I could do. The data skills tutor respected my decision and assured me of their ongoing support during this challenging period. It was heartening to know that my difficult return to education after all these years was met with understanding and empathy, yet I would much rather keep my struggles with maths private.

Initially, I felt low, inadequate, and vulnerable. However, I had to regain control and turned to my seventeen-year-old son, seeking his assistance. I needed to understand the complexities of percentages, mean, mode, median, ratios, decimals, and problem- solving techniques, but I simply could not do it alone. My brilliant son willingly agreed to help, and for several days, we sat together, working through practice papers tirelessly. Our joint efforts paid off: I finally felt that I had mastered the mathematical concepts that had for so long evaded me. I felt equipped to confidently tackle the data skills practice questions. My comprehensive review of mathematical concepts was supported by a textbook called *Business Maths Brief*. A pivotal moment arrived when my classmates and I faced an online mathematics test with a strict ninety-minute time limit. I participated without hesitation, though internally I was horrified, and achieved an exceptional score of 96% out of 100. This achievement was even more unforeseen, considering that just a few weeks prior, I was akin to a closed and bewildered book, silently observing my tutor and classmates without having an answer to even the simplest of mathematical problems.

With the dedicated support from my son, over just a few days, I not only caught up with, but also outperformed some of my classmates, who had been confidently answering questions during classes. Where previously I had compared myself to the other students and felt myself lacking, I now felt like we were equals. My son had broken the hold my GCSE Maths teacher had held over me for so long. It's worth noting that teaching in the correct manner, showing examples of each mathematical rule so that every student understands, is fundamental. After all, every student's capabilities are different. My 'Data Skills' tutor, who understood that I was struggling but never belittled or judged me, was one such teacher. I was brave enough to share my limitations with them and this allowed them to provide the highest level of support, though I never directly asked them for the extra help. This ensured that I didn't back out and instead built enough confidence and resilience to pass the module with flying colours.

After completing the online data skills class, I openly wept. With support from my family and my tutor, my personal weakness had become my personal triumph. I finally realised that it is okay to ask for external assistance and to embrace the help of others.

As part of the 'Data Skills' Module assignment, I was required to write a report addressing the outcomes of investigations conducted among three medical centres. The objective was to select a medical centre that could serve as a model for others and provide the most practical benefits. In this task, I worked with numerical data, creating pie charts and bar graphs. My existing knowledge of Microsoft Excel was poor, and I struggled to understand how to create charts and graphs. This became evident in front of the class, but during a one-on-one feedback session, my tutor again corrected my mistakes and patiently showed me how to use Excel and input numerical data. Suddenly, it was as though a lightbulb had been turned on. I persevered and managed to write the report independently. In the end, my efforts paid off. I achieved an overall score of 70% in the Data Skills module, equivalent to an 'A' grade. Alongside this achievement, I completed all of the Semester 1 modules by mid-December 2020, passing every subject, casting away personal doubts, and learning as much about myself as I did about the topics covered.

Semester 2

The surge in COVID-19 cases during December 2020 and January 2021 was alarming, echoing the national fear and confusion that had gripped the UK during the initial outbreak in March 2020. Lockdown measures were reinstated, and the fear of leaving the house resurfaced. The world grappled with combating the virus and safeguarding our lives. This time, my family did not remain unaffected. I lost two close family members, and grief gripped our household. However, as the saying goes, "The show must go on." I mourned my loved ones but knew that I had to continue on with my life, which meant that my studies take place, despite the ache of my loss.

In mid-January 2021, I embarked on the second semester of my foundation year. I once again adapted to working from home, managing my family responsibilities, and pursuing my degree online. This semester introduced new modules, each with a new schedule: 'The Pitch Project' was held on Tuesday and Thursday evenings from 6:00 p.m. 'Global Debates' was conducted on Saturday mornings, and 'Research Skills 2' was scheduled for Saturday afternoons. By now, with the chaos that had rippled globally since the start of 2020, I had become conscious of my ability to quickly adapt to new routines, realising flexibility and organizational skills were a key part of this process, and thankfully, came naturally to me. I added these elements of my personality to the growing list of personal strengths that I had identified since starting my degree, knowing that they would be valuable qualities in my professional pursuits. My academic journey continued with these new modules, offering a blend of learning experiences.

Research Skills 2

In the first semester, 'Research Skills 1' seemed straightforward, and I achieved an 'A' grade without encountering any significant hurdles. However, 'Research Skills 2' proved to be more of a challenge. Understanding and mastering the necessary skills for the assignment briefing was difficult. These skills included grasping the thesis, middle arguments, and conclusion. The topic was critical: writing an essay that examined factors related to Social Cognitive Theory (SCT) in application, using a case study from Royal Bournemouth and Poole Hospital. Social Cognitive Theory (SCT), originally known as Social Learning Theory (SLT), was developed by Albert Bandura in the 1960s (Sutton, 2021). It later evolved into SCT in 1986. This theory emphasises that learning occurs within a social context, involving dynamic and reciprocal interactions among three key factors: personal, environmental, and behavioural (Partridge 2008):

- **Personal Factors** include an individual's self-efficacy, personality, and values. Self-efficacy refers to one's belief in one's ability to perform specific tasks or achieve goals. Personal factors play a crucial role in mental, emotional, and theoretical functioning (Persson, R. et al., 2014).

- **Environmental Factors** are influences that shape personal factors and vice versa. The environment can be either supportive or challenging, affecting individuals' emotional experiences and actions. For instance, a positive or negative environment can trigger different emotions and lead to various behavioural responses (Collins et al., Higgs 2019).

- **Behavioural Factors** arise from an individual's social context, including their social support system and external pressures. People are socially influenced to modify their behaviour, often conforming to social norms or expectations (Persson, R. et al., 2014).

For this assignment, my classmates and I delved into academic journals, rather than relying solely on the textbooks that we had encountered in 'Research Skills 1.' The teacher emphasised that journals are primarily authored by researchers, professors, and experts, with a specific focus on academic and technical audiences rather than general readers. This concept was new to the entire class, myself included. Journals provide a wealth of information, often starting with an abstract that outlines what to expect in the rest of the article. The typical structure of a journal article includes sections such as 'Introduction', 'Methods', 'Results', 'Discussion', and finally, 'Conclusion.' The following are a few journal articles that aided me in completing my Research Skills 2 module assignment:

- *Assessing the Determinants of Internet Banking Adoption Intentions: A Social Cognitive Theory Perspective* (Published in Computers in Human Behaviour): This article explored factors influencing people's intentions to adopt Internet banking, drawing from social cognitive theory.

- *Two Observational Studies Examining the Effect of a Social Norm and a Health Message on the Purchase of Vegetables in Student Canteen Settings.* This research investigated how social norms and health messages impact vegetable purchasing behaviour among students.

- *The Relationship Between Self-Efficacy and Help Evasion* (Published in Health Education & Behaviour). This study explored the connection between self-efficacy and the resistance to accepting assistance from others.

I also gained valuable insights from a case study conducted by Anglia Ruskin University, which focused on the Virtual Learning Environment (VLE) at Royal Bournemouth and Poole Hospital. Various other journal articles enriched my understanding and significantly contributed to my successful completion of the assignment. Despite the initial complexity of the task, my proficiency in English topics had always surpassed other skills. I knuckled down, creating a draft for feedback from my tutor. Although the initial version wasn't exceptional, and my tutor acknowledged that improvements could lead to higher marks, they informed me of my passing grade based on the draft alone. Ultimately, I achieved a secure 'B' grade, and this experience provided novel insights into Albert Bandura's Social Cognitive Theory (SCT), which has many practical applications in our lives.

Global Debates

In my second semester, the 'Global Debates' module quickly became my favourite so far. This intriguing and challenging topic conjured images of spirited debates within the hallowed halls of Parliament, where politicians engage in intense verbal battles. The class format was engaging: the teacher assigned a topic and all students, including myself, presented arguments based on our personal viewpoints. It was an exhilarating experience, but at its core, the module emphasised the importance of well-researched information. We were encouraged to back our arguments with firm Harvard-style referencing, ensuring that our speeches carried weight even in the face of opposition. The teacher provided a diverse array of practice topics, spanning from "Diversity and Positive Action in the Workplace" to themes centred around sustainability or social influences. The textbook that aided both the tutor and students was titled *A*

Rule for Arguments. However, the pinnacle of my journey was the final debate: "Can countries or governments be run like companies or businesses?" I excelled in this thought-provoking discussion and secured yet another 'A' grade— though this time I had been confident in my performance from the start.

It was during this module that I found pride in my natural ability to stand my ground and convey my views. I have never been someone who shies away from debate, particularly when it comes to topics I am passionate about, but I hadn't previously connected this part of myself to success in a business environment. The tomboyish streak from my childhood, combined with my abba's emphasis on the importance of letting my voice be heard, came flooding back, proving to be valuable tools during this module. The thrill of rebutting during the final assignment fuelled my enthusiasm. Many people, especially traditionally women, doubt the value of their voice, or their right to make themselves heard. Standing your ground with a well-informed argument in the face of opposition is a difficult life skill to harness but is an imperative part of success. Perhaps my affinity for creating and enforcing persuasive arguments was what had, in my youth, fuelled my desire to become a lawyer, and it was now something I could finally find a purpose for.

I would have loved for the Global Debates module to continue beyond the foundation year of my degree, but the skillset I had polished during these studies was already proving beneficial in the full-time job I held whilst studying.

I was able to apply these more refined debate techniques to my role in sales, boosting my success in persuading customers to agree to my terms during transactions.

The Pitch Project

In the final module of semester two, I encountered 'The Pitch Project.' This project closely resembled the TV show *"The Dragon's Den,"* where entrepreneurs pitch their proposals to a panel of business experts. The focus was on highlighting both the advantages and disadvantages of the business idea, with a strong emphasis on the positive aspects. The proposal included detailed information on 'The 4 Ps' of marketing, otherwise known as the 'Marketing Mix:' products, price, place, and promotion. Along with this came a comprehensive overview of the financial requirements necessary for business expansion. 'The Marketing Mix' is a term used to refer to the key areas to focus on when developing a marketing plan - there is a longer version of this formula, known as 'The Seven Ps,' which includes people, packaging and process. However, for this assignment, we were asked to look at the four key elements used. The ultimate goal was to convince potential investors that the business held significant potential, encouraging them to provide essential financial support for its growth.

Entering this module felt like an exhilarating leap into the business world, embracing the well-known concept of pitches with excitement. We were all aware of *"The Dragon's*

Den," so we naively felt confident that we knew what it took to develop a successful pitch. However, during the 'Pitch Project' module, I encountered an unexpected and formidable challenge. The difficulty stemmed from our group work, which involved three members of the class working as a team. Initially, I felt confident about joining my group. Our task was to create a presentation outlining our business plan across three key areas, which seemed simple enough.

Each team member assumed a specific role: The Chief Executive Officer (CEO), The Chief Marketing Officer (CMO), and The Chief Financial Officer (CFO). I chose to be the Chief Marketing Officer, recognising my weakness in mathematical areas and my lack of familiarity with the specific duties of a Chief Executive Officer. I had learned how to embrace my strengths and weaknesses, so I opted for this role, knowing that it wouldn't require me to significantly contribute to the financial responsibilities of a CFO or take on the leadership role of a CEO.

Our group developed a fictional business plan that led to the creation of 'AJH Medical Solution LTD,' a unique concept that involved the placement of vending machines located in London tube stations. Our primary focus was to offer authorised over-the-counter medication to all travellers who may require immediate or emergency treatment during their journeys. Our product range would include pain relief items, first-aid supplies, and essential personal protective equipment (PPE) like face masks and hand sanitisers - particularly relevant during the COVID-19 pandemic. This innovative venture's aim was to efficiently address the health needs of travellers as and when they might arise.

Yet again, I encountered my reoccurring hurdle: my group members excelled in mathematics, while I still struggled a little in that area. They adeptly handled the financial aspects of the business plan, leaving me feeling like a less capable contributor. It was a disheartening experience. As they worked on the financials, I sat online, feeling inferior and useless, with memories of my struggles in 'Data Skills' during semester one playing in my mind. Though they did not purposely exclude me, I found myself lacking the confidence to join in, and they automatically took the reins.

While my son had supported me with the basics back in 'Data Skills,' the 'Pitch Project' involved more business-related financial calculations, which he couldn't assist with. What he had taught me during that period, however, was the power of my resilience and determination to learn. I reclaimed my positive mindset, knowing that if I could handle the rapid learning I had thrown myself into back in the 'Data Skills' module, I would find a way to overcome this hurdle, too.

I replaced my doubts with optimism, recalling my abba's wisdom: *"Tough times are transient. Rather than surrendering, seek alternative solutions to overcome challenges, knowing that darkness eventually gives way to light."* So, leveraging my strength in English, I made valuable contributions to the overall business plan, focusing on my areas of expertise and acknowledging my limitations. In the final analysis, I excelled—the result of a meticulously prepared presentation and a well-crafted business plan. I drew inspiration from the book *Now Build a Great Business (7 Ways to Maximize Your Profits in Any Market)*, written by Mark Thompson and Brian Tracy in 2011. My efforts were rewarded with a 'B' grade for the module.

Having successfully completed the foundation year, I was awarded an overall grade of a 'High B' for my efforts. I now held an open ticket to embark on the journey toward an International Business Management degree. I now not only possessed newly acquired insights into the mechanics of a successful business, but also newly acquired insights into myself. As I studied 'Professional Communications,' I realised the value of finding experience-based abilities that had previously gone unrecognised. During the 'Data Skills' module, I learned my ability to quickly learn a new skill, as well as the power of perseverance. 'Global Debates' taught me how to use personal passions as strengths, whilst with 'The Pitch Project' I found an understanding of how to use my identified strengths to counter my weak points. With new-found confidence, I was ready to plunge myself deeper into the world of higher education.

As the final three months before the next stage of my education—the first year of my full degree—unfolded, I found myself cocooned in the warmth of summer. The sun, a steadfast companion, bestowed a golden glow upon everything it touched. In this summer of contentment, I surrounded myself with loved ones, knowing that the memories created would endure long after the season's petals had fallen. It became a precious time to savour before embarking on the rigours of the upcoming academic year. While I found studying for my university degree fascinating, the constraints of time often hindered my full enjoyment of moments with family and friends. Though I understood that with any form of success comes some level of sacrifice, I knew that it also came with much bigger rewards. The reward for sacrificing my already limited free time during those months of study was now a new-found appreciation of the simple things and small moments that bonded us. A bigger reward, however, was the casting aside of the previous summer's anxiety, replacing it with self-assurance and an eagerness to learn more. The narrative remained incomplete - my journey toward success was only just beginning, teeming with hope, courage, and novel opportunities. I was poised to conquer challenges and defy the odds.

Chapter References:

Alexander, B., Adams Becker, S., and Cummins, M. (October 2016). *Digital Literacy: An NMC Horizon Project Strategic Brief.* Volume 3.3. The New Media Consortium. https://eric.ed.gov/?id=ED593900.

Beyene, S. (2012). Language skills: way to get up? *The Guardian.* London, Guardian News and Media Limited.

Boateng, H. et al. (December 2016). *Assessing the determinants of internet banking adoption intentions: A social cognitive theory perspective.* Science Direct. https://www.sciencedirect. com/science/article/abs/pii/S0747563216306446#: ~:text=Drawing%20inspiration%20from%20the%20 social%20cognitive%20theory%2C%20we,of%20 use%2C%20compatibility%20with%20lifestyle%2C%20 online%20customer%20service.

Bolt, M. and Dunn, D.S. (2016). *Pursuing Human Strengths (A Positive Psychology Guide).* 2nd edition. Worth Publishers.

Briken, K. et al. (2020). *The New Digital Workplace: How New Technologies Revolutionise Work.* Red Globe Press.

Cleaves, C., Hobbs, M., and Noble, J. (2014). *Business Maths Brief.* 10th edition. Pearson Education Limited.

Collins, E. I.M., Thomas, J. M., Robinson, E., Aveyard, P., Jebb, S.A., Herman, C.P., and Higgs, S. (January 2019). *Two observational studies examining the effect of a social norm and a health message on the purchase of vegetables in student canteen settings.* Science Direct. https://www.sciencedirect.com/science/article/pii/ S0195666318305890.

Cottrell, S. (2015). *Skills for Success: Personal Development and Employability.* 3rd edition. Palgrave.

Partridge, H. (October 2008). *Redefining the digital divide: Attitudes to matter.* Asist. https://asistdl.onlinelibrary. wiley.com/doi/10.1002/meet.1450440251.

Persson, R. et al. (February 2014). *The Relationship Between Self-Efficacy and Help Evasion.* Pubmed. https://pubmed. ncbi.nlm.nih.gov/23345337/.

Rook, S. (2019). *The Graduate Career Guidebook.* 2nd edition. Red Globe Press.

Sutton, J. (May 2021). *What is Bandura's Social Learning Theory? 3 Examples.* Positive Psychology. https:// positivepsychology.com/social-learning-theory-bandura/.

Thompson, M. and Tracey, B. (2011). *Now Build a Great Business!: 7 Ways to Maximize Your Profits in Any Market.* Amacon Publishing.

Weston, A. (2017). *A Rule for Arguments.* 5th edition. Hackett Publishing Company, Inc.

Chapter Three:

First Year

In mid-September 2021, my anticipation felt like pins and needles as I prepared to embark on the first year of my International Business Management degree. The world, still recovering from the echoes of lockdowns and pandemic heartache, had shifted its classrooms to virtual realms. Zoom sessions were still replacing lecture halls, smudgy screens were standing in for face-to-face interactions.

Though my studies had begun the previous year, that had been my foundation year—an equivalent to, and replacement for, the A-Levels I had never obtained in my youth. Its purpose was to prepare me for the upcoming work I would be doing during my full degree, and teach me the basics I would need to know to get started. Now, venturing into the first year of the degree course had me bubbling with enthusiasm. I had come to realise that in the same way my foundation year had been to prepare me for the upcoming course, my degree itself would be the foundation upon which my future would be built. To me, this wasn't just the start of a degree - it was the ignition of my capabilities.

While the pattern of online classes remained the same, the beginning of this year felt different. This time around,

I stood at the starting line, chomping at the bit and ready to throw myself into my studies. The personal growth I had achieved during my foundation year had allowed me to cast away the doubt in my capacity to learn that had marred the start of my journey into higher education. It felt exhilarating. I felt powerful. I sensed equality—standing alongside my peers, who, despite all of our differences in backgrounds and life experiences, I now felt I shared similar capabilities with. The feeling of inequality had not been a stranger to me. As the child of immigrants, as a Muslim, as a woman, as someone who, despite my best attempts, was considered by others as an academic failure. When the time came for my classmates and I to step into the first year of our degree, I finally felt as though I truly had just as much to offer and achieve as everyone else. Out of the rollercoaster of victories and setbacks I experienced during my foundation year studies with Anglia Ruskin University, accepting that I deserved success was the biggest lesson. All of us, regardless of our background, deserve success. Sure, some of us have to work harder than others. The playing field is not equal. The starting point is not the same. The hurdles differ in size. But, embracing these facts and understanding that we have the right to achieve what we desire just as much as the next person is the first step to success.

Beneath that excitement, however, lay a quiet ache - a void that echoed with memories of my abba. Abba, the unwavering presence who had held my hand through childhood, instilled bravery in my bones and whispered resilience into my soul. He was the beacon of unwavering support, the one who believed that every tempest held a glimmer of light that would become a guiding star. At times, I would find myself subconsciously echoing his teachings. Though admittedly, my patience level doesn't match abba's. I can become frustrated quickly, and my irritation is not always easy to hide, but our values are steadfast and parallel. Yet, somewhere along the line, despite sharing his wisdom with my own children and those around me, I had forgotten to apply it to myself. He had stood by me, a silent pillar of strength, whispering, *"Fear not, move forward,"* but somehow, I had become stagnant. His certainty that every problem has a solution had seen me support others in the search for answers to their own problems, but never to mine. I had remained true to his teachings, passing his wisdom on to others, but now I realised that I had not stayed true to myself and my potential, and it was time to rectify that. His presence, like a comforting shadow, once again assured me that no obstacle would be insurmountable. His words suddenly resurfaced, swirling in my mind, proving that they had etched themselves onto my heart. I recognised that I must be calm. Let my soul be still. Obedience to my abba's belief in patience became my compass—returning me to my path toward success.

This unwavering belief had been his greatest weapon for his own success. He placed great importance on higher education, given that he had been deprived of any form of schooling during his childhood. For him, education wasn't merely a personal pursuit - it stood as a legacy to cherish. Despite his own illiteracy, he recognised the value of learning and made it a priority for all his children. His encouragement and support allowed me and my siblings to pursue both academic studies and religious education. He shared with us his spiritual journey, encouraging us to use ancient verses to guide us. I treasure the memory of reciting the Quran when I turned ten, with Abba sitting beside me quietly, letting the pride he wore on his gentle face speak for him.

Yet, life's cruel twists had snatched him away, leaving me with an emptiness that no degree could fill. I longed to share my triumphs with him, to tell him that I was stepping into the halls of academia, ready to conquer the world. His pride would have been immeasurable, his chest swelling with joy. *"My daughter,"* he would have said. *"Not just an undergraduate, but a force to be reckoned with."* Despite knowing that I would never hear those words, I instead let my mind return to those days when his face spoke for him. I recognise the privilege of having such a parent – that many people never got to experience the grace of a patient role model. I realised that having the guidance and wisdom of a mentor such as my abba is something that gives me an advantage. Where some may come from a background with financial benefits, and others may have been granted academic achievements to give them the upper hand, I had been given the gift of my abba's faith in me as my tool for success. His words were not given to me for me to simply pass them on to my children. It was time to reclaim his teachings and apply them to myself, as he had intended. The years see all of us lose cherished people in our lives, and it is difficult at times to accept that they won't be there to witness significant moments in our lives, but the best way to honour their memory is not to lament, but to triumph.

Semester 1

As I prepared to harness my newfound confidence and plunge into the first semester of year one of my degree, two modules in particular caught my attention. The first being 'Academic and Professional Skills,' which would focus on study skills, research methods, and effective communication. The second was the 'Business and Environment' module, which would delve into the internal and external factors that influence businesses, including innovation, micro and macro environments, research, and technology trends.

Academic and Professional Skills

To kick off my degree's first year, I was presented with an intriguing project for my 'Academic and Professional Skills' module. We were tasked with crafting a report titled 'Analyse the impacts of making a city centre car-free.' The assignment's audacity caught my attention. It seemed like an impossible aim, the logic seemed elusive, and the reality far-fetched. My mind flung up memories of a Bollywood movie I had seen at some point or another: *Love Story 2050.* The plotline involved futuristic cities with flying cars and no need for roads. At the time, the concept had fascinated me, despite being a fanciful work of science-fiction. My imagination had been captured by this notion, and the mystery of where technology would one day lead us. Perhaps the film wasn't pure fiction - maybe it hinted at transformation and innovation ahead. I realised the symbolism and how it echoed the assignment. Not flying cars, perhaps, but indeed a harbinger of change.

The assignment suddenly became exciting, taking the seemingly impossible goal, and finding a solution to the problem. The assignment involved evaluating strategies to enhance the advantages and mitigate the difficulties associated with transforming a city centre into a car-free zone. This subject was a novel area of inquiry for me, presenting an opportunity to harness my creative side, and investigate the dynamics of establishing a car-free urban core. Innovation is at the heart of a successful business, so it became apparent to me the significance of the task and its relevance to the course.

To comprehensively address the assignment, I consulted various scholarly articles, with a key resource being the journal article *Stakeholder Impact Analysis in Construction Pro-*

ject Management' from *The Field of Construction Management and Economics* written by Stefan Olander in 2007. Though the topic of construction had previously been something that was of little interest to me, the article drew me in. An analysis of the economic impact reveals a strong link to employment, which is essential for economic development. Business impacts are also intertwined with employment and contribute to economic growth, making the relevance of the piece clear. From my research, I found that Olander (2007) suggests stakeholders may feel both positive and negative effects, reflecting their diverse interests.

For instance, daily car commuters might struggle with the shift to more localised jobs. Conversely, urban residents stand to gain from the proliferation of job opportunities that accompany the adoption of green policies. This shift towards sustainability, as noted by Bowen & Kuralbayeva (2015), explores an eco-friendlier cityscape in the absence of cars. When it comes to analysing business impacts, local authorities must engage a variety of stakeholders, such as businesses and residents, in discussions prior to the execution of plans for car-free urban areas (Rydningen et al., 2019). This ensures that the perspectives of business owners are taken into account, that the initiative is in line with economic growth objectives and in the best interest of those it may impact. The reduction of vehicular congestion paves the way for a more inviting urban atmosphere, enriched with facilities like malls, eateries, and leisure spots

(Rydningen et al., 2019). These existing studies revealed that, in essence, the transition to car-free cities presents a conducive environment for business prosperity and economic advancement. With my new understanding of the topic, the report I prepared meticulously outlined the primary stakeholders impacted by the shift towards a car-free city centre. The analysis of this report was structured into three distinct segments: economic impacts, environmental consequences, and social effects.

Another finding was the concept of grade separation as a strategy for developing a car-free city. I learned that approach involves aligning transportation routes at different heights, but further research revealed that the financial burden of building underground routes can be substantial, which is something crucial to consider when exploring viable options (J.H. Crawford, 2002). Another possible avenue is housing developments designed to minimise dependency on cars, emphasising sustainable architectural designs, materials, and energy consumption, which may be a more practical tactic as far as economic impact goes (Kushner, 2005).

When exploring the environmental benefits of reducing the number of cars on the road, I realised from my extensive research that this approach addresses the critical issues of pollution and climate change are addressed, noting that motor vehicles are major contributors to air pollution, CO_2 emissions, and global warming. The establishment of car-free cities is seen as a means to enhance air quality, public health, and the environment at large (Glazener-Khreis, 2019). For the section on social impact, I explored the concept that getting rid of cars could lower the chances of serious crimes such as 'road rage.' This term refers to harmful behaviours, whether physical, psychological, or emotional, directed at others in the driving environment. Road rage is often a result of frustration or anger, with factors such as irresponsible driving or congestion coming into play. A reduction of cars on the road would mean a reduction in these incidents, thus avoiding the physical or emotional harm that can be experienced by victims of such crimes (Cavacuiti et al. Locke, 2013). Furthermore, it's argued that replacing roads with green spaces could lead to less crime by promoting community and reducing hostility, creating an overall positive social impact.

Yet, there were negatives to think about when developing this theory. I realised that the opposite effect could unintentionally be a result, with the misuse of these spaces for crimes such as drug dealing or gang formation creating dangerous environments, rather than community assets. Racial or ethnic segregation, opportunities for crimes, and overall hostile community dynamics could form, should these spaces be misused (Bogar et al. Kirsten, 2016).

Weighing up the pros and cons of each aspect of the segments in the report was critical. This allowed me to use my initiative and develop recommendations and suggestions designed to tackle the impacts various strategies for change may incur. I had to take into consideration elements such as business and employment, financing, education, and community impact in order to make valuable proposals. I understood that the purpose of this task was to teach us the importance of doing extensive research, exploring hypothetical outcomes, and collecting relevant data when forming any kind of business plan or change.

My initial fascination with the concept of creating a car-free city captured my imagination as soon as the task was revealed, and I believed that it would be a straightforward project that simply required imagination. When I received initial feedback, however, it was not as strong as I had hoped, which shook my confidence, especially since I had put so much effort into extensive secondary research and collecting data to analyse. Despite the sting of the criticism of my report, I delved into reviewing and improving the content of my report and finishing the assignment to the best of my ability. I realised that enthusiasm about the topic wasn't enough, and that it needed to be backed more firmly with a well-written piece, which, through perseverance, I was eventually able to produce.

Though I delivered an excellent report, my self-assurance had been knocked. I knew that if I did not shake off my disappointment and prove my capabilities - to myself more than anyone else - I could very easily slip back into the self-doubt I had worked so hard to leave behind. I decided that rather than feel sorry for myself, I would dust myself off and push myself further. I opted to take on the task of giving a group presentation titled 'How can managers enhance corporate social responsibility?' I had hoped that I would be able to stop my bubbling anxiety in its tracks by balancing my disappointment with achievement, so despite an already packed schedule, with full-time work and family duties, I knuckled down and dedicated every second of my spare time to research and data collection. As I logged into Zoom to begin my presentation, I suddenly felt out of my depth. I had worked so hard on this, but I had stretched myself too thin, trying to force a well-rounded piece of work into too little time. My teacher noticed this, and my dependence on my notes was picked up on, resulting in a lower mark than I had hoped. My attempt to claw back my sense of worthiness had backfired. My overall grade was decent, but my enthusiasm was marred. I realised that I still had a lot to learn. Accepting my disappointment with grace was difficult, but throwing in the towel at the first hiccup was simply not an option.

Business Environment

My first semester had not got off to a great start, but learning from past mistakes is all part of progress, and I had to keep my chin up. "Keep calm and carry on," as they say. 'Business Environment' promised to be another challenging module. The focus: the concept of 'The PESTLE Analysis'. This acronym stands for political, economic, social, technological, legal and environmental factors, all of which hold sway on the success of a company. The first assignment for this module was to create a practical presentation that emphasised the importance of education in providing new intellectual insights. My chosen focus company, Rolls-Royce, was more than just a luxury car brand - it operated across land, sea, and air as a leading provider of power systems and services. Initially, I had been oblivious to this element of the company, but through in-depth secondary research, I learned details that expanded my understanding of their multifaceted business operations, allowing me to apply this lesser-known information to my presentation.

However, the complexities of PESTLE analysis bogged me down. Getting my head around the multiple angles that are imperative for decision-makers to keep in mind wasn't as straightforward as I had expected. The various factors overlap in unexpected ways, resulting in a myriad of issues that may befall those who call the shots. This time, I approached the task with caution, asking my online module tutor for guidance rather than attempting to tackle it independently. The mistake in my previous module was to throw myself into the assignment with enthusiasm alone, thinking that I had a full understanding without checking first. After the feedback I received on that project, I at first felt that better examples and demonstrations from my tutor would have made a difference, but I realised that I had never asked for them. Assuming that I was receiving all the guidance that I needed without actually checking had been my downfall, and I refused to make the same blunder twice. With patience, my tutor helped me pick apart the complexities of the PESTLE analysis, taking on board their feedback to create a comprehensive presentation, this time achieving an 'A' grade. The purpose of the PESTLE analysis itself is to help those who make decisions for a business to avoid jumping in head-first without ensuring that they have a full understanding of the factors in question, and I noted how this mirrored my own experience. Of course, those who call the shots in a company at times need to ask for the advice of experts, and this reflected the valuable lesson I learned the hard way—collaborative learning is key.

Following the presentation, the module required we produce a report investigating innovation in contemporary businesses and applying these concepts to a real-world company, Hikma Pharmaceuticals PLC—a British multinational pharmaceutical firm. My research explored how innovation influences business growth and efficiency, citing examples of modern organizations using innovation to improve performance and gain a competitive edge through new technologies and automation. For both the presentation and the written assignment, I referenced two primary texts: *Management: Using Practice and Theory to Develop Skills*, eighth edition, by David Boddy, published in 2019, and *Business in Context: An Introduction to Business and its Environment*, 7th edition, by David Needle and Jane Burns, also published in 2019. Innovation plays a role in product launches, overcoming design hurdles, securing financing, and making incremental improvements in areas such as advertising and management strategy to meet customer demands. From my trawling through the journals and books that were key to my research, I found that some companies rely on the creativity of their scientists and engineers to develop new pharmaceuticals and automotive engineering solutions (Boddy, 2019).

A case study of a florist entrepreneur highlighted the importance of innovation in leveraging social media platforms and creating a high-quality website to attract clients, proving that creatively harnessing current trends and modern communication methods offers a significant advantage to businesses (Boddy, 2019). While innovation involves research and development costs, it offers more benefits than drawbacks in complex and competitive business landscapes (Needle and Burns, 2019).

In my study of Hikma Pharmaceuticals PLC, I examined their innovative strategies and market responsiveness. The company provides a wide array of over 780 premium medicines, featuring a diverse collection enhanced by an extensive in-licensed product strategy (Hikma and Model, 2021). This strategy involves agreements between two companies, where one becomes the 'in-licenser,' and the other the 'out-licenser.' In-licensing involves a company acquiring rights to a product, technology, or intellectual property from another organisation. This allows the licensee to expand its portfolio and access innovative resources without developing them in-house. Out-licensing involves a company granting rights to its product or intellectual property to another organisation, which pays royalties or fees. It is a strategic and effective revenue-generating arrangement (Pharmablog, 2023). Hikma's innovative business approach is founded on three strategic pillars: first, to maximise the potential of their established medical injectables business, second, to develop a portfolio of innovative products that anticipates future health needs, and third, to engage and earn the loyalty of their employees (Hikma, 2024).

I then went on to examine business ethics and Corporate Social Responsibility (CSR) in contemporary businesses, again focussing on Hikma Pharmaceuticals' PLC. Business ethics involves understanding right and wrong within business contexts, emphasising moral obligations towards organisations, stakeholders, and broader societal roles, known as corporate social responsibility. It enhances decision-making standards at both individual and organisational levels. Four key areas include behavioural ethics, technological ethics, virtue ethics, and the impact of unethical leadership. Stakeholder theory posits that businesses should value all stakeholders, not just shareholders, recognising the importance of both primary stakeholders (customers, employees, investors, suppliers) and secondary stakeholders (competitors, laws, governments) in influencing business operations (Crane and Matten, 2016) (Wasieleski and Weber, 2019) (Freeman, 2018) (Cragg, 2002). Hikma Pharmaceuticals PLC's ethical framework is built on seven core principles that reflect their commitment to stakeholders and corporate social responsibility. These include ensuring the highest quality in all aspects of business, being a reliable and responsive partner, respecting human rights and privacy, upholding integrity by avoiding fraud, fostering employee development and safety, maintaining transparency in business reporting, and actively contributing to community welfare and environmental sustainability (Hikma Code of Conduct, 2023).

My project proposed strategies to foster innovation, maintain ethical integrity, and uphold corporate social responsibility within Hikma Pharmaceutical Ltd. I included two recommendations in my assignment. The primary suggestion I put forward involved developing cutting-edge technological equipment to potentially reduce reliance on partnerships as Hikma and their associate company Arecor (Arecor.com) expand their collaboration through a new agreement aimed at creating and marketing ready-to-administer medications (Hikma, 2024a).

Arecor is a biopharmaceutical company with a global focus. Their mission is to improve patient care by developing innovative medicines. The company achieves this by enhancing existing therapeutic products using their proprietary formulation technology platform called Arestat™, which offers several advantages in the development of pharmaceutical products (Arecor, 2024). Arecor, specifically, works on creating stable, injectable, high-concentration formulations for their trademarked products (Arecor, 2024). As such, the partnership agreement between Arecor and Hikma was a logical step for the companies' growth, and an innovative connection that would greatly benefit both companies.

My second recommendation emphasised ethical and corporate social responsibility. Hikma, as a pharmaceutical company, can manufacture and support patients in developing, economically poor, and non-industrialised countries, such as South Sudan and Central African Republic (Third World Countries, 2024). By doing so, they can provide essential healthcare to populations who cannot afford treatment. This approach will enhance Hikma's business ethics and their corporate social responsibility efforts, potentially increasing their competitive advantage.

Delving into these subjects deepened my grasp of contemporary business operations, highlighting elements of international business that I had previously had no understanding of. My hunger for this information surprised me, never before realising that not only did I want to take a stab at making it in the field of business management, I desired to eventually be running my own business, calling the shots, implementing innovation, and producing a business with ethics and social corporate responsibility. I imagined applying the Stakeholder Theory Model to something I was proud of, not just part of. I became aware that the degree didn't simply have me engaged — I was inspired and invested.

Perhaps my imagination got the better of me during my first semester, and though I excelled in the module's presentation itself, my resulting overconfidence, especially following the knock I had felt during my 'Academic and Professional Skills' module, saw me overlook a detailed review of my written assignment tasks. Following this feedback, I knew I had to rectify the issue. Rather than getting ahead of myself and dreaming of running a business in the future, I applied my focus to the learning I still had to do. I confidently completed my final report in only three days, landing myself just a few marks short of an 'A' grade.

With a breath of relief, my first semester was over. Despite finding the assignments significantly more challenging than those in my foundation year, both modules—'Business Environment' and 'Academic and Professional Skills'—sat neatly behind me, with grades I was quite pleased with overall, though I was aware of the room for improvement. By this time, it was mid-December 2021, and the break in my studies, despite brief, was enough for me to get some respite. I was still juggling my existing full-time work, and responsibilities as a mother and homemaker, but I used this time to reflect on the studies of my first semester and the knowledge I had received. As winter embraced London, I embraced a sense of pride—a feeling new to me. Of course, I had often experienced pride. Pride in my children. Pride in my family. But this time was different. This time, I was proud of myself. I had already achieved so much more than I ever expected to, as sixteen-year-old me sat weeping in my bedroom, clutching another set of GCSE results that branded me a failure. At that point, I had truly believed that my education was over, never imagining that it could possibly start again, even all these years later. In mid-January 2022, my one-month break came to an end, and I prepared to start the second semester of my first-year degree. The respite had done me good, giving me the chance to process how far I had come.

Semester 2

I needed very little personal preparation for my second semester. In fact, I had been eagerly waiting the day my studies would resume, and I could once more log in to the virtual learning platform that I had become so familiar with. Being halfway through my first year of my degree was a place more of comfort than uncertainty. By now, I had developed my routine and had adapted to the requirements of my studies. I felt less out of my depth and more able to balance my time.

There was not an ounce of worry about the rest of the year. I knew that I was due to face some unexpected hurdles, but learning to expect the unexpected and navigate my way around whatever was thrown my way was a skill that was blossoming for me. When the time finally came, I settled at my computer, notebook at the ready, and clicked the link that would open the next chapter of my studies.

Business Finance

'Business Finance,' which required those dreaded mathematical skills, was connected to 'Data Skills'—a topic I had encountered in the first semester of my foundation year. This was the module that had seen me call on my son's support, cramming our free time with numbers, equations, and statistics that would swirl around my head like wasps, buzzing and bothering me. I knew that I was capable and now equipped with a basic understanding, but nevertheless, trepidation gnawed at me. The thought of applying what I had only recently learned to an entirely unfamiliar subject like economics was nerve-wracking, but also surprisingly exciting.

On the first day of my online 'Business Finance' class, we had an introductory session. When it was my turn, I introduced myself by sharing my name, employment position, and family background. However, I also openly admitted that my mathematics skills were extremely poor. I felt exposed and vulnerable, putting my shame so openly bare to strangers. I had to push the words out, past the lump in my throat and reveal this 'dirty secret' to the class. Though forced, showing my vulnerability was a calculated decision. My intention was to unburden myself and let my teacher know that I may need extra support, giving them the opportunity to pre-empt my struggles and spot when I may be steering off track before I went too far in the wrong direction.

Learning, whether it be in an academic setting or in the wider world, can be a two- way street. In order to let my teachers do their job properly, I had to be honest about my weaknesses. I had to let them know where I may need them to hold my hand through a topic, regardless of the embarrassment I still held about it. Though asking for help when encountering difficulties is something I had by now learned was part of the journey, asking for support beforehand was a new tactic for me, and one I had hoped would pay off.

The initial assignment centred around constructing a cash budget for a company, a topic we had already studied in previous classes. We were tasked with exploring the best way for a made-up company called 'Kashi Textile' to control their finances over three months, including elements such as outgoing utility bills, receipts for purchases of items such as new computers, and regular expenses such as delivery charges and accountancy fees. By exploring all of the potential outgoings of the business, we then had to decide how to allocate existing funds from the opening sales balance of each month to each area effectively. I completed this section without any trouble, lulling me into a sense of security. The subsequent assignment questions shifted to literacy-based topics, a format I was much more comfortable with. For my first assignment, I primarily relied on the scholarly book *Accounting: A Smart Approach* by Mary Carey and Cathy Knowles (2020).

Our next focus was the definition of a company, as well as company features, with advantages and disadvantages when forming a public company. This topic was new to me, so I invested considerable time in reading to grasp the meanings of various business and company-related terms. Here are my understandings:

A company is a legal entity registered under the 'Companies Act,' with various forms such as limited or unlimited companies, private or public companies, and community interest companies (Pahwa, 2021). Additionally, based on my interpretation, the features of a company can include:

- **Incorporation**: A company becomes legally recognised when it registers under the Companies Act (or equivalent laws). To achieve this status, it must fulfil requirements related to documents (such as Memorandum of Association and Articles of Association), shareholders, directors, and share capital.

- **Artificial Legal Person**: A company is treated as an artificial legal entity. It can acquire or dispose of property, enter contracts, and engage in legal proceedings.

- **Separate Legal Entity**: A company operates independently from its members or controllers. It is responsible for repaying creditors and facing legal actions. Individual members are shielded from personal liability for the company's actions.

- **Perpetual Existence**: Unlike some non-registered business entities, a company enjoys stability—it continues to exist regardless of changes in membership.

- **Common Seal**: Companies use a common seal (bearing the company's name) as an alternative to signatures. This seal represents the company's authority in legal matters.

- **Limited Liability**: Companies can be limited by shares or by guarantee. Shareholders in a limited company risk only the amount they've invested; their personal assets are protected from company debts.

- **Incorporated Association**: When a company registers under the Companies Act, it is officially established. Relevant documents provide details about the company's name, directors, objectives, and internal rules (Pahwa, 2021).

Advantages of public companies include the ability to raise funds through stock sales to the public, while disadvantages involve adhering to government reporting standards during an Initial Public Offering (IPO) (Public Companies, 2023).

Next, I delved into the importance of cash in business, and whether it serves as a reliable indicator—a relatively straightforward concept that I wrapped my head around quite swiftly. Cash is vital for businesses. It encompasses actual cash, bank balances, and short-term deposits. Obviously, having enough cash is crucial for paying suppliers, employee wages, loan interest, and dividends. Without sufficient cash, even profitable businesses can collapse. In essence, cash is the lifeblood that enables businesses to meet financial obligations promptly (Carey and Knowles, 2020).

I discovered that profit alone is not a reliable indicator of cash balances. Both cash flow and profit are crucial for maintaining continuous financial performance in companies (Stobierski, 2020). Profit (or net income) is the remaining amount after deducting all costs from revenue, whereas cash flow measures the actual movement of money into and out of a business over a specific period. Positive cash flow indicates that more money is entering the business than leaving it, while negative cash flow shows the opposite. This means that profit doesn't always correlate directly with cash flow. In summary, while profit is crucial for long-term growth, cash flow ensures short-term survival. Businesses need both (Stobierski, 2020) (Carey and Knowles, 2020).

Corporate governance principles and the definition of 'gearing,' along with its associated advantages and disadvantages, were the next part of the assignment. I learned that corporate governance establishes rules for UK companies, ensuring efficient direction and control. It promotes long-term stakeholder relationships and holds directors accountable for acting in the company's best interest (Carey and Knowles, 2020). The principles of good governance are:

- **Company Culture Alignment**: The Board of Directors should ensure that the company's culture aligns with its purpose, principles, and strategy.

- **Stakeholder Communication**: Companies should engage with a wide range of stakeholders (suppliers, customers, local community) to build confidence.

- **Employee Engagement**: The Board should actively listen to employees' views.

- **Merit-Based Appointments**: The Board appointments should follow a formal, transparent process based on merit.

- **Transparent Remuneration**: Clear procedures should determine directors' pay. Companies must report on governance principles in their annual reports. (Carey and Knowles, 2020).

Lastly, I explored why banks take an interest in a company's level of gearing, giving me an insight into economics that most people have never even considered. 'Gearing in financial' measures how much a company relies on debt versus equity for financing. 'High gearing' means more debt, while 'low gearing' indicates more equity funding. When a company relies more on debt (such as loans or bonds) to fund its operations, it has higher gearing.

The advantages of gearing are:

- Debt is a more affordable source of finance, and gearing can benefit shareholders when the company is generating increasing profits and trading successfully (Carey and Knowles, 2020).

- Companies are not solely dependent on retained profits and ordinary shares for expansion. Geared companies can raise capital through loans and debentures —a type of long-term business debt not secured by any collateral (Carey and Knowles, 2020).

The disadvantage of gearing is that highly geared companies carry risks for ordinary shareholders, including reduced dividends and potential insolvency if debt obligations aren't met.

The most notable disadvantages of gearing are:

- **Dividend Risk**: Profits may be insufficient for dividends after interest payments.

- **Insolvency Risk**: Lenders can force bankruptcy if interest obligations aren't fulfilled. (Carey and Knowles, 2020).

As I progressed through the 'Business Finance' module, I encountered a final assignment—the one I had been dreading. We were presented with an online mathematics test that covered concepts from financial accounting to management accounting. Practical tests during the last class sessions helped me to grasp the material, and all students had access to online practice tests to prepare for the final two-hour exam. Determined not to relive my exam failures, I diligently reviewed these resources, focusing on the areas where I struggled most—the mathematical problem-solving questions. The combined effort of practising at home and preparing online during classes boosted my confidence. Finally, I sat the exam. I had expected to feel much worse than I did; anticipating sweaty palms and a head full of fuzz, but the fervour with which I had prepared had granted me a calmness and unforeseen sense of sureness in my ability.

As each question was answered, I was one step closer to discovering exactly how much I had truly come to understand mathematics, especially when linked to business. When the test was complete, though I was relieved, I also was uncertain what the outcome would be. I had performed to the best of my ability and could do nothing but wait to receive my grade to find out if it had been enough. I had to make a conscious effort not to worry about this, knowing that it was now out of my hands.

Navigating the 'Business Finance' module was initially daunting, particularly with the knowledge that mathematical complexities were heading my way, like a ten-foot wall ready to stop me in my tracks. I had envisaged myself desperately scrabbling at the bottom of this imaginary wall, struggling to find any footing amongst the tangle of numbers and equations that formed the barrier, blocking my path. However, forewarning my teacher of my concerns and allowing them to identify areas in which I may need extra guidance gave us both the opportunity to brace for potential stumbles, and I was able to soar over this hurdle, sensing the wall crumble behind me, finally defeated. I now understood that pre-empting potential hurdles and sourcing support where needed is something needed as much in personal development as it is in the business world. The bashfulness with which I had initially broached the issue was unnecessary; the value in anticipating issues, and with support preparing for them, was clear.

As I wrapped up the module, the final marks for both written and practical components left me beaming: an 'A' grade. Only weeks ago, I had been bracing myself for disappointment. Perhaps a 'C,' at best. Most likely lower. It felt that I had turned the seemingly impossible into reality, conquering the odds that had once seemed stacked against me. I had accepted that I simply lacked natural ability when it came to mathematics, but even this could be outdone with preparation and determination.

Economics of Business

At first glance, 'Economics for Business' resembled a cryptic puzzle – its hidden shapes shrouded in mystery. Yet, as I delved deeper into this academic realm, I discovered that 'Data Skills' and 'Business Finance' adhered gracefully to mathematical rules. Their steps were predictable, their rhythms familiar. But Economics? Economics spun in enigma. It defied rigid equations, favouring the fluidity of prose and the elegance of graphs. I struggled to grapple with the intricacies of supply and demand—the elusive curves that weave the fabric of economic reality. The supply curve revealed how much goods or services sellers were willing to offer at different prices. The demand curve mirrored buyers' desires at those prices.

Together, they danced, finding equilibrium where buyers and sellers converged. And then, more steps emerged: Marginal costs slipped in—the expense of producing one more item. Income Elasticity and Price Elasticity joined the choreography, measuring people's sensitivity to changes. At times I yearned to vanish into the digital ether, escaping the perplexing equations. But I persevered, using my newfound understanding of mathematical rules, twirling through the complexities, and forcing myself to join the dance. As the first week of the module unfurled, I found myself presented with a seemingly unrealistic challenge: an online assignment that had been introduced to the class.

This time, however, it didn't seem like it was just me who was struggling. Like my peers, I found myself staring at the screen, attempting to interpret the cryptic instructions provided by the teacher. The sense of confusion was palpable, but at least I wasn't drifting alone in this sea of uncertainty. The three assignment questions approached us like an impenetrable puzzle—the hardest I had encountered since my foundation year.

This time, I sought the guidance of an online private tutor to unravel the meanings behind critical economic concepts. Almost reflective of the topic, I knew that paying a tutor for extra support was an investment. Despite full-time work, my financial means were not limitless, with the responsibilities of parenthood taking the central focus of my outgoings, but I knew that investing time alone would not be enough. I was grateful that I had this privilege, aware that this kind of investment is not an available option for everyone in my position, but I had recognised the opportunity and the need to take it. In an extensive tutoring session, we delved into the intricacies of resources, scarcity, and cost-benefit analysis.

My new mentor illuminated the path, clarifying the true essence of each of the assignment questions and the specific type of answers required to conquer the module. The questions that had plagued me with sleepless nights now felt less haunting. I knew that understanding these fundamental principles would be my compass, guiding me through the maze of economic reasoning. The assignment was not just about answering questions - it was about unravelling the intricate web of economic concepts and applying them to real-world scenarios. I emerged from the tutoring session armed with newfound clarity—a guiding light to navigate the challenging waters of microeconomics. Outsourcing external assistance had been worth the associated cost, proving to be an asset I had certainly needed to invest in.

Empowered by my private tutor's insights, I delved into further reading. The once bewildering terms now made sense, and I gleefully connected the dots, letting the puzzle fall into nothingness. My trusty companion on this journey? The textbook, *Essentials of Economics*, by Paul Krugman and Robin Wells (2020). As I eagerly turned the pages, my confidence blossomed, allowing me to set sail through the once turbulent waters of economic understanding, no longer adrift without a paddle.

The three questions I addressed to complete this Economics for Business assignment were as follows.

- My first question required me to explain how resource scarcity and opportunity cost influence microeconomic decision-making for households and individuals in the UK.

Figure 1: Opportunity Cost= Next best alternative foregone

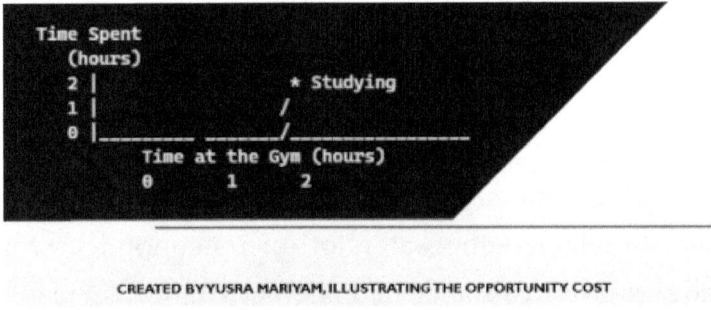

```
Time Spent
  (hours)
   2 |                    * Studying
   1 |                   /
   0 |_____ _____/_____
        Time at the Gym (hours)
          0       1       2
```

CREATED BY YUSRA MARIYAM, ILLUSTRATING THE OPPORTUNITY COST

In **Figure 1**, the concept of opportunity cost is displayed:

- **Studying**: Represents the hours spent studying.

- **Time at the Gym**: Represents the leisure time given up at the gym due to studying.

- **Point on the Graph**: Indicates the trade-off between studying and spending time at the gym.

It shows how opportunity cost applies to the next best alternative that is foregone when making a decision. For instance, in this example, the opportunity cost of studying for 2 hours is the leisure time you would have spent at the gym. Another example might be spending £100 to attend a live game. The opportunity cost of this choice is the other things you could have spent that £100 on, like purchasing your favourite clothes, or taking an inexpensive holiday.

Figure 2: Increasing Opportunity Cost

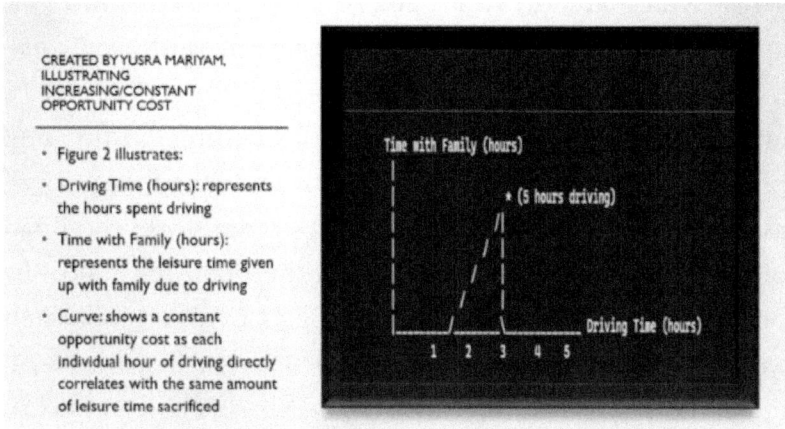

CREATED BY YUSRA MARIYAM,
ILLUSTRATING
INCREASING/CONSTANT
OPPORTUNITY COST

* Figure 2 illustrates:

* Driving Time (hours): represents the hours spent driving

* Time with Family (hours): represents the leisure time given up with family due to driving

* Curve: shows a constant opportunity cost as each individual hour of driving directly correlates with the same amount of leisure time sacrificed

This diagram helps visualize the trade-off and opportunity cost between spending time driving versus spending leisure time with family.

Opportunity cost, central in economics, arises from scarcity. Scarcity implies that resources like money, time, or labour are limited. We can't have everything we want, so we must make choices. For instance, with £20, we could buy an economics textbook or have a meal at a restaurant. Each choice involves a trade-off—the value of what we give up by not choosing the alternative (Pettinger, 2019). Another example is spending £50 on an expensive cinema ticket. The opportunity cost is what you could have done with that £50, like having a family lunch or dinner. Each choice involves a trade-off for the alternative option.

In the UK, there has recently been a shortage of human capital, which encompasses a worker's economic value based on experience, education, training, intelligence, and skills (Krugman and Wells, 2020). Between 2019 and 2021, approximately half of UK companies encountered challenges related to human capital scarcity due to COVID-19 and Brexit. Recruiting new staff and retaining existing employees became particularly difficult during this period, as highlighted by Partington, (2021). Therefore, the head of education at KPMG emphasised the need for action by businesses and the government. KPMG UK is a global network of independent professional services firms that offer audit, legal, tax, and advisory services. Their expertise spans various domains, making them a significant player in the professional services industry (KPMG, 2021) (Partington, 2021). To counter the issues surrounding the human capital shortage, their goal was to reskill and upskill potential workers in order to address the growing skills gap in the workforce. By doing so, they aimed to prevent the UK's economic recovery from slowing down (Partington, 2021). Essentially, this approach involves using the concept of opportunity cost – the value of the next best alternative - as a recovery strategy to combat the scarcity of human capital. Failing to address shortages of highly skilled and professional employees could negatively impact the economy.

- My second question required me to explain how cost-benefit analysis and incentives influence microeconomic decision-making for households and individuals in the UK.

Cost-benefit analysis involves evaluating trade-offs when making significant decisions. It entails comparing the costs associated with a specific action against the benefits of an alternative choice. For example, when choosing a subject to study, an individual might prioritise the one that aligns better with their needs, considering its potential benefits. An incentive refers to anything that encourages behaviour modification. It provides opportunities for individuals to enhance their wellbeing or receive rewards. Lastly, a marginal decision involves choosing slightly more or less of an activity, such as making trade-offs at the margin (Krugman and Wells, 2020).

As I had experienced myself, navigating the complexities of childcare costs can indeed be challenging for working families, particularly parents who juggle professional responsibilities with raising young children (Letters, 2019). However, the UK's government provides a childcare support system that involves various programs across different departments (Official Statistics, 2021). Free Entitlement is where all children are entitled to fifteen hours of funded childcare per week from the term after they turn three years old. Working families can access up to thirty hours. Vulnerable children (or those in the poorest 40% of families) start their fifteen-hour entitlement at age two. The Tax-Free Childcare scheme allows families to pay for childcare from pre-tax income.

For every £8 parents pay into the Tax-Free Childcare account, the government adds £2, up to a maximum of £2,000 per year per child. Disabled children receive more support, with the government contributing up to £4,000 per year. The Universal Credit Subsidies provide lower income working families support through the benefits system, with subsidies covering up to 85% of childcare costs for those on universal credit (Official Statistics, 2021). However, these are all incentives for working parents provided by Government contributions, that will encourage parents to continue working. The expansion of these provisions during the COVID-19 lockdown to include self-employed parents enables working parents to make informed decisions about their careers while managing household budgets (Official Statistics, 2021).

Economically, this government intervention can lead to an increased demand for money, as parents allocate funds for childcare expenses. As a result, we observe a rightward shift in the money demand curve, reflecting the changing financial landscape for working families (Krugman and Wells, 2020).

I realised that researching and critically evaluating the question, then finding the answers based on thorough research, was as interesting as it was important. With the help of my tutor, applying more focus to the question in order to understand all implications of it made my research easier and more accurate, rather than muddling around in the dark in the hope that I was heading in the right direction.

This process revealed real-world applications, such as the complexities of childcare, the economic implications of government intervention programs, policy analysis regarding the effectiveness of various programs, the social impact of supporting working families, behavioural economics related to incentives, and issues of equity and accessibility in providing support to lower-income families.

Figure 3: Shifts of Demand Curve

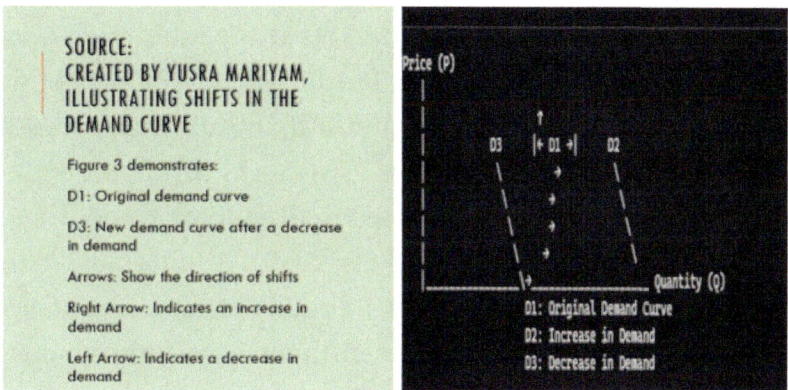

SOURCE:
CREATED BY YUSRA MARIYAM, ILLUSTRATING SHIFTS IN THE DEMAND CURVE

Figure 3 demonstrates:

D1: Original demand curve

D3: New demand curve after a decrease in demand

Arrows: Show the direction of shifts

Right Arrow: Indicates an increase in demand

Left Arrow: Indicates a decrease in demand

D1: Original Demand Curve
D2: Increase in Demand
D3: Decrease in Demand

Increase in Demand (Shift to D2): This occurs due to factors such as higher consumer income, increased popularity of the product, or a decrease in the price of complementary goods.

Decrease in Demand (Shift to D3): This happens due to factors like lower consumer income, decreased popularity of the product, or an increase in the price of complementary goods.

- In the final question, I needed to analyse and explain how the market economy leverages consumer habits, such as cost-benefit analysis and the desire for incentives, to drive business profits.

According to the government, in market reports from 2009, markets function as structures for managing resources. Efficient competitive markets have the potential to enhance consumer welfare and contribute to economic growth. This, in turn, leads to an overall increase in total welfare. Therefore, it is crucial for markets to operate effectively. When markets function well, businesses thrive by meeting consumer demands at a lower cost than their competitors. Effective competition benefits consumers through greater choices, lower prices, and improved quality of goods and services (Government in Markets, 2009). Additionally, businesses strategically use price reductions and incentives, such as Black Friday sales, to influence consumer behaviour (Race, 2021).

A notable example of an incentive is demonstrated by the British multinational clothing brand Next, which specialises in clothing, footwear, accessories, and homeware (Next, 2024). Next is a brand I am particularly familiar with, as I regularly shop in their store and online. However, according to a BBC News report (2019), Next faced significant challenges due to increased competition on the high street, and cautious consumer spending amid Brexit uncertainties. Despite these challenges, Next adapted by shifting its focus to online sales. By encouraging consumers to shop on their website, Next saw strong sales in the weeks leading up to Christmas. This strategic move allowed them to capitalize on the broader trend toward internet-based shopping. This implies that Next carefully weighed the costs and benefits when deciding to prioritise online sales. Additionally, this introduced an incentive for consumers to shop on their website rather than in physical stores. Personally, I found their online shopping experience to be seamless and convenient and often opted for shopping from their website over visiting a store in person.

Being a busy mother of six made shopping trips difficult, and this became doubly difficult when I also began my full-time job, so using a website that is user-friendly and benefitting from a prompt delivery service allowed me to continue purchasing their goods, even when life was busy. I came to realise that my personal experience when moving my shopping habits online was part of their tactical business decision, which had been a solid success. This also opened my eyes to the fact that all of my shopping experiences have been part of carefully researched and planned processes, with Next being just one example of this.

After finishing my written assignment by addressing the three questions, I later reflected with some frustration. Despite feeling quietly confident in the work I had produced, guided by the insights I had received during the session with a private tutor, I felt that as a student, I would have benefitted from a clearer starting point. Though my module teacher had tried to provide explicit instructions and illustrative examples for each question, it didn't quite fit my learning style, so I was left with a murky understanding of what I needed to produce. Each student possesses unique abilities and learns in a different way, and unfortunately for me, this assignment felt just beyond my reach, leaving me in need of further support. I could have saved time and money if the work had happened to be presented in a way that worked in time with my often-whirring brain, but I had to accept that it simply wasn't a good fit for me, so I had to use my initiative and find an alternative solution. I chose to take the experience as a lesson, realising how—almost ironically—my decision to make an investment had reflected the topic itself.

My next challenge in the 'Economics of Business' module was a presentation. The assignment? To compare the UK's CO2 emissions per capita with those of Switzerland— a nation known for its low environmental impact. I was tasked with creating a five-minute presentation titled Why does the UK exhibit high CO2 emissions (CO2e), and how could it learn from Switzerland to reduce this environmental burden? Undeterred, I immersed myself in thorough research, consulting a multitude of secondary sources. I wrestled with data, theories, and policy implications, weaving together a holistic comprehension. Empowered by fresh insights, I confidently addressed the presentation with the following answers:

The UK's carbon footprint, measured in greenhouse gas emissions (GHGE), reached its peak in 2004. However, by 2018, it has decreased significantly, standing at 31% lower than the 2004 peak. The main contributors to the UK's greenhouse gas emissions from 1996 to 2021 are imported goods and services. This is followed by UK-produced goods and services consumed by UK residents, UK households heating arising from the use of fossil fuels, and UK transport emissions generated directly by UK households (Gov. UK, 2021).

Learning from Switzerland, the UK could focus on the following strategies to reduce greenhouse gas emissions:

- Invest in more research and development, leveraging Switzerland's expertise in this area. Develop and implement updated digital solutions to further reduce emissions.

- Address energy consumption and heating practices in households to achieve emission reductions (Gov. UK, 2021) (Switzerland's Long-Term Climate Strategy, 72021) (HM Government, 2021).

After completing this presentation, I gained new insights into greenhouse gases and the contrasting approaches of Switzerland and the UK in reducing emissions. Overall, the topic was fascinating, and the doubt and confusion that had initially swamped me when I began the module had been replaced with a transformed understanding. The graphs, terminology and theories fell neatly into place, I was able to convey my findings clearly and focus without fear on the assignment, finding that I actually enjoyed the module and the new information it had provided me with.

The outcome? Despite a rocky start, I had triumphed, completing the 'Economics for Business' module with a respectable 'B' grade. Yet, my experiences through the module held a more personal lesson - sometimes, knowledge of answers alone is insufficient. The true puzzle can lie in comprehending the questions themselves. For students, understanding the context and nuances of each query is paramount. Equally crucial is the role of teachers—ensuring that students grasp the essence of the challenges set before them. It had been strangely comforting at the start of the module, realising that my peers were faced with equal confusion. In previous assignments, I had even envied them, feeling as though I was alone in my difficulties, but the realisation that I was not solitary in my struggles had driven me harder than envy ever had. Something about knowing we were all facing varying levels of perplexity, that I wasn't simply stupid or lacking, had been a gift. As it turns out, we are never truly alone, or the only person in the room who doesn't quite comprehend a challenge.

I experienced a compelling urge as I approached the conclusion of the 'Economics for Business' module. The idea of delving deeper into economics and potentially becoming an Economist suddenly fascinated me. This was something I had never expected from myself—the blur and tangle of economics had transformed into something I could actually see myself pursuing as a career. The true beauty of each academic module reveals itself when mastery is achieved. Answers seem to hover in the air, waiting to be discovered, no longer out of reach. I noticed that, somehow, I had inspired myself—the courage I had mustered out of nowhere forming a mosaic of determination, dedication, and the desire to achieve. I hoped that I myself one day could serve as a light for all who strive to unravel the mysteries of learning. I had discovered the conqueror within me, one that I had never known was there. With my first year sitting neatly behind me, I found myself hungry for more.

Over the course of the first year of my degree, I navigated both positive and challenging experiences across four modules: Academic and Professional Communications, Business Environment, Business Finance, and Economics for Business. While some assignments and presentations posed no issues, others were more difficult, and I needed to outsource extra support to overcome the challenge.

Despite these obstacles, I persevered, explored alternative approaches, and drew inspiration from my abba's teachings—to remain patient and seek solutions, rather than to simply give up. The gift of his wisdom remains my unwavering support, something I am grateful for each day. Just as I have drawn strength from that one crucial factor, I encourage others to persevere in challenging situations. Though it can sometimes be hard to find, all it takes is steadfast determination to unravel the puzzle and overcome obstacles.

Chapter References:

Murray, A. (January 2025). *Next sales boosted by late Christmas Surge.* Business Live. https://www.business-live. co.uk/retail-consumer/next-upgrades-profit-forecast-christmas-30724767.

Adams, K. (October 2021). *Net zero strategy: Build back greener.* ASBP. https://asbp.org.uk/asbp-news/net-zero-strategy

BODDY, D. (2019). *Management: Using Practice and Theory to Develop Skills.* 8th edition. Harlow, England.

BOGAR, S. and BEYER, K. (March 2015). *Green Space, Violence, and Crime.* ResearchGate. https://www.researchgate. net/publication/274319355_Green_Space_Violence_ and_Crime_A_Systematic_Review.

BOWEN, A. and KURALBAYEVA, K., 2015. [online] *LSE.ac.uk*

Carey, M. and Knowles, C. (2020). *Accounting: A Smart Approach.* 4th edition. Oxford University Press.

Cavacuiti, C., Ala-Leppilampi, K., Mann, R., Govoni, R., Stoduto, G., Smart, R. and Locke, J., (December 2013). *Victims of Road Rage: A Qualitative Study of the Experiences of Motorists and Vulnerable Road Users.* ResearchGate. https://www.researchgate.net/publication/260250364_

Victims_of_Road_Rage_A_Qualitative_Study_of_the_
Experiences_of_Motorists_and_Vulnerable_Road_Users

Cragg, W. (2002). Business Ethics and Stakeholder Theory. *Business Ethics Quarterly,* 12(2), pp. 113–142. doi:10.2307/3857807.

Crane, A. and Matten, D. (2019). *Business Ethics: Managing Corporate Citizenship and Sustainability in the Age of Globalization.* Oxford University Press.

Crane, A. and Matten, D. (2016). *Business Ethics.* Google Books.

Crawford, J.H. (September 2002). Carfree cities: Articles: J.H. Crawford: An idealized design for carfree cities and its application in the real world. Carfree.com. https://www.carfree.com/papers/crawford_imcl.html

Freeman, R.E. (2018). About. Alt Text.

Glazener, A. and Khreis, H. (January 2019). *Transforming Our Cities: Best Practices Towards Clean Air and Active Transportation.* Springer Nature Link. https://link.springer.com/article/10.1007/s40572-019-0228-1

Government in markets (2009). Government in markets.

Gov. UK (May 2024). *Carbon footprint for the UK and England to 2021.* GOV.UK. https://www.gov.uk/government/statistics/uks-carbon-footprint/carbon-footprint-for-the-uk-and-england-to-2019

Gov.Uk. (November 2021). Skills and Post-16 Education Bill: Policy Summary Notes. Gov.Uk.

Department of Education. https://assets.publishing.service.gov.
uk/government/uploads/system/uploads/attachment_
data/file/1035459/Skills_and_Post-16_Education_Bill_
November_2021_policy_notes.pdf.

Gov.UK. (August 2021). Tax-free childcare statistics
commentary June 2021.

GOV.UK. https://www.gov.uk/government/statistics/tax-free-
childcare-statistics-june-2021/tax-free-childcare-statistics-
commentary-june-2021.

Hikma (2024). Strategy, Hikma.

Hikma (2024). *Hikma and ARECOR expand collaboration with new
agreement to develop and commercialise ready-to-administer
medicine.* Hikma. https://www.hikma.com/news/
hikma-and-arecor-announce-exclusive-agreement-to-
develop-and-commercialise-ready-to-use-medicine-using-
arestat-technology/#:~:text=The%20product%2C%20
which%20will%20be%20announced%20prior%20
to,to%20deliver%20new%20reformulations%20of%20
existing%2C%20complex%20products.

Hikma Code of Conduct (2023). Hikma Code of Conduct.

Krugman, P. and Wells, R. (2020). *Essentials of Economics: Fifth
Edition.* Amazon.com

KUSHNER, J., 2005. Car-free housing developments: Towards
sustainable smart growth and urban regeneration
through car-free zoning, car-free redevelopment,

pedestrian improvement districts, and new urbanism. [online] *Thefreelibrary.com*

Letters (2019). Expensive childcare holds families back | letter. *The Guardian.*

Needle, D. and Burns, J. (2019). *Business in Context: An Introduction to Business and its Environment,* 7th edition. Cengage Learning EMEA.

NEXT (2024) *At a glance, – Next Plc.*

OLANDER, S., 2007. Stakeholder impact analysis in construction project management. [online] *Taylor & Francis.*

Partington, R. (2021). UK employers struggle with worst labour shortage since 1997. *The Guardian.*

Pahwa, A. (August 2023). *What Is a Company? Meaning, Features, & Types of Companies.*

Feedough. https://www.feedough.com/what-is-a-company-meaning-types-features-of-a-company/

Pettinger, T. (March 2019). *Opportunity cost definition.* Economics Help. https://www.economicshelp.org/blog/2177/economics/opportunity-cost-definition/

Pharmablog. (May 2023). *In-licensing vs out-licensing in the pharmaceutical industry.*

Pharma Venue. https://www.pharmavenue.com/blog/pharma-info/in-licensing-vs-out-licensing-in-the-pharmaceutical-industry/

Public Companies (2023) *Public companies, Corporate Finance Institute.*

Race, M. (November 2021). *Black Friday: Which? warns over price offers.* BBC News. https://www.bbc.com/news/business-59380453

Rydningen, U., Hoynes, R. and Kolltveit, L. (June 2017). OSLO 2019: A Car-Free City Centre. Research Gate. *https://www.researchgate.net/publication/320220711_OSLO_2019_A_CAR-FREE_CITY_CENTRE*

Stobierski, T. (April 2020). *Cash Flow vs. Profit: What's the Difference?* Harvard Business School Online. https://online.hbs.edu/blog/post/cash-flow-vs-profit.

Third World Countries 2024 (2024) World Population Review, Third World countries 2024.

Switzerland's Long-Term Climate Strategy (2021). Switzerland's long-term climate strategy.

Wasieleski, D. & Weber, J. (2019). *Business Ethics.* Emerald Publishing Limited.

Chapter Four:

Second Year

After a long summer break, September 2022 arrived, bringing with it the end of the chaos that the pandemic had rocked the world with. And, as such, it was time for the end of online learning. The world was no longer confined to digital interactions, and university doors swung open for face-to-face classes. For me, this was not a transition 'back to normal,' but the start of a brand-new experience that was as exciting as it was nerve-wracking.

My entire experience of education as an adult had been online, with both my foundation year and year one of my degree spent safely behind a computer screen. Though I knew it would happen sooner or later, the prospect of sitting in a physical classroom felt like a daunting challenge. My last encounter with face-to-face classes was during my disastrous GCSEs, and the idea of re-entering that environment stirred a blend of emotions—some good, others terrifying. I had become accustomed to sitting at my desk at home, logging in and learning in the comfort of my own environment. I had never even stepped foot in a university classroom, imagining the huge lecture halls, as seen in American movies, a sea of faces, no doubt all much younger than me, looking like they truly belonged there. The fear of facing classmates and teachers loomed large in my mind. I wondered how I would cope with the live lectures, the bustling classrooms, and the social interactions. In my school years, I had always sat at the back of the class, trying to be invisible, hoping not to be called upon by the teacher. I would make myself small, dreading the sound of my name leaving my teachers' lips and landing all eyes on me, exposing my lack of understanding in front of my peers. Now, as a mature student, I contemplated whether I'd still gravitate toward the back or if I had developed enough confidence during my online classes to venture closer to the front and make myself known. I had a strong suspicion that the mortified high school student within me would win this tug-of-war, and that I would slip easily into the desire for obscurity. Despite my age, I felt once more like a child, lost and confused in the face of their first day at school.

I carried an additional burden—the mild stammering that surfaced when extreme nervousness struck. The prospect of speaking in front of a room triggered anxiety, a large rock dropping in my stomach at the very thought. Online, I had been able to disguise my stammer by taking a moment to compose myself or attempting to slow down my speech. The safety of my own home kept my anxiety low, letting me speak in front of the class during presentations without feeling the eyes of my peers boring into me. But now, this safety had been stripped away, and the thought of this was unnerving. How would I manage my speech? How could I push down that anxiety and prevent the dreaded stammering from surfacing? These thoughts weighed heavily, especially now, feeling that as an adult I should have already overcome the complications. Granted, I had been self-managing my stammer and had developed coping mechanisms over the years, but I also felt as though the expectations of someone my age would be higher. That people would expect a person with life experience to have the confidence that comes with it. But my life experience involved raising my children, supporting them in their education, and going to great lengths to ensure that they had the opportunity become graduates and pursue careers they loved. My life experience did not involve speaking to large audiences or performing presentations in person. I hoped that judgement would fall differently now than it had in the 1990s during my high school years, but I had no way of knowing.

Semester 1

On the eve of my first day of in-person classes, I laid awake, mind racing. Though I was excited to resume my studies, I was apprehensive. The faces I had spent two years staring at through screens swarmed my mind. Though I knew the names, knew the faces, they were still strangers. Online learning left no room for getting to know my peers. No time for small talk or invites to grab a coffee after class. I was aware that they might not be who they seemed online, and aware that to them, I might not be who I seemed, either. After what felt like endless months of lockdown, social distancing, and the remote working and learning situations that lay in the wake of the COVID-19 pandemic, I realised that, like many others, I had been made an involuntary recluse. Meeting new people and adapting to a new social life was an exhilarating idea, but one marred with uneasiness. In my head, I remembered Allah (god), and then my abba's words. "You'll be fine—no need to feel fear. Remember, I'm here with you." His words always differed from the rest, those simple words, etched into my memory since childhood. "No need to feel fear"—my new mantra. Granted, he was no longer here with me, but his words will remain within me until I too am gone.

After a turbulent sleep, I stood at the doors to the university building, feeling like a statue, with excited students buzzing around me. I'd been in university buildings before, accompanying my children as they considered their education options and prepared for exciting futures. Back then, I was the proud parent of a student. This time, it was different. This time, I *was* the student, standing at the threshold of my future. This time it was about me—Yusra Mariyam— reaching for *my* dreams. Many years had passed since the crushing end of my early education. Marriage, managing a household, cooking for six hungry children, and then six hungry teenagers, full-time work, and now, finally, the pursuit of higher education. Standing there, in the reception of the university, I questioned myself. *Is this true? Is it really happening? Is this a cruel, taunting dream? A ghost of my academic shortcomings?* I knew that I had to stamp down those negative thoughts, but that is much easier said than done. I had come too far to back down now. Bowing out and letting those negative thoughts win would be a much easier path, returning to the way things had been before and the comfort of the familiar. *Abba* had taught me that the easiest or most comfortable path never leads to the destination we deserve. He had led by example, not just words. The many struggles of his life, his hard work, and the tough decisions he had to make all culminated to form a man who inspired those around him. I knew that this was a moment for me to lead by example, and to hopefully inspire someone in some way. My legs felt as though they could take on a mind of their own and send me running from the challenge, but instead, I mustered the courage to make them approach the reception desk.

With directions from the receptionist, I navigated the maze of corridors that led to my classroom, lost in thoughts about the challenges I had conquered during the first year of my degree, and those unknown challenges I was about to face in my second. I was snapped out of my stupor by some almost-familiar faces. Seeing my classmates in 3D for the first time added to the surrealness of the moment, but reality hit me—I had to acknowledge that it was truly happening, and that I truly deserved it. I realised that I wasn't alone in my emotions; other students also grappled with fears and uncertainties. Though many of my peers seemed confident, choosing their seats and chatting with ease, I noticed that many seemed to share my anxiety. We all exchanged awkward glances, attempting to recognise each other from our online sessions, and offering tentative introductions. The room was a lot less intimidating than I had imagined. In fact, it was quite welcoming. Clearly, Anglia Ruskin University had created a space for learning, not simply to cram as many bodies as possible into one room. Nervous but determined, I chose a seat. While the front row seemed too audacious for me, I settled into the second row, parking myself at an empty desk on the left side of the room. This seemed close enough to engage, but not so close that I drew attention to myself. It felt as though everyone else knew the drill—pulling out laptops or notebooks and pens, preparing to take notes. I copied, trying to follow a crowd who seemed to know what they were doing but were probably equally as nervous as me. After all, I had to remind myself, it was their first day, too. I was not the only one.

Within moments, a poised gentleman walked into the room, his warm smile captivating our attention and hushing the room. He introduced himself, revealing that he would be teaching the module, 'Legal Aspects of Business.' The class sat silently, yet the air seemed to buzz with anticipation as we readied ourselves for our inaugural in-person class. We listened tentatively as our new teacher ran through what we should expect for the coming semester, and what would be expected of us in return.

As for this semester's schedule, we had the following modules:

- Legal Aspect of Business: Saturday mornings
- Sustainability in Career Development: Saturday afternoons
- Human Resources Management: Tuesday and Thursday evenings at 6 p.m.

And just like that, it was time to hit the ground running.

Legal Aspect of Business

I found the 'Legal Aspect of Business' module intriguing, stirring memories I had long dismissed. Back when I was studying for my GCSEs, I harboured a desire to pursue a law degree—a dream that remained unfulfilled. Though I had let this dream fall from my mind long ago, the content of this module struck a chord with me. Each Saturday, I eagerly participated in discussions, immersing myself in the subject matter with fervour. It felt like the chance to rewrite the narrative and embrace the disappointments, knowing that they had led me to my current path and this wild adventure. Admittedly, I had conflicting emotions. Though I was thoroughly enjoying the lessons, I wondered how different things might have been had I passed those few GCSEs back in the 1990s. Perhaps then, A-levels would have followed, leading me toward a legal career. I felt a sadness for my younger self, knowing now how that girl would have felt, enjoying studying the intricacies of law and legalities. The experience added depth to my story, reminding me that life's twists and turns often land us exactly where we need to be. Reality reminded me how fortunate I was to be a university student, albeit decades later than I would have liked, and in a different field. However, even in my new field—business—understanding laws remains crucial.

The module's teacher added a unique touch to the experience. His skill in captivating the entire class made Saturdays feel like a welcoming space where I truly belonged. I wasn't alone in my enjoyment - the entire class seemed to appreciate the engaging and inspiring atmosphere he fostered. Delving into the 'Legal Aspect of Business' module shone a light on various topics at the intersection of law and business. Within the module, I encountered a diverse range of topics, supported by the textbook *Business Law* authored by James Marson and Katy Ferris (2020). Here are some key legal terms that I have learned and understood:

- **English Legal System**: Understanding the legal framework in England. The focus lies on describing and evaluating the institutions and personnel engaged in the practice and administration of justice. This includes an examination of courts, tribunals, and the reasoning behind their authority.

- **Contract Law**: Delving into the intricacies of contracts, their formation, and enforceability. Managers often handle contracts that bind the organisation, so understanding contract law is crucial for those in this position. This can include offer and acceptance in agreements, consideration, intention to create legal relations, and certainty of terms.

- **Agency Law**: Exploring the relationships between principals and agents. In numerous business transactions, a third party interacts with an agent who represents the principal. For example, when a customer buys coffee from a high-street chain (the principal), they engage with the staff at the counter (the agent). Both the principal and agent have specific duties and responsibilities.

- **Business Organizations Law (Company Law)**: Learning about different business structures and the various forms of business organisation available to traders. These options range from sole proprietorships to partnerships, as well as incorporation as a limited liability partnership (LLP), private limited company, or public limited company (PLC). Each structure has its own advantages and disadvantages for both members of the organisation and external parties. Considerations include taxation, succession planning, and regulatory implications (Marson & Ferris, 2020). Additionally, when organisations become incorporated, they transform into artificial entities, known as corporations. Upon incorporation, they gain their distinct legal personality. The most prevalent example of such entities is a limited company.

I found this particular area of business and company law intriguing and found myself driven to explore it more. I came across a fascinating case that allowed me to develop more insight into the concept, which is as follows:

In the landmark legal case of Salomon v Salomon & Co. Ltd (1897), significant principles of company law were established. We explored this specific case in detail, picking apart the story that went with it. Mr. Salomon, a successful leather merchant, had operated as a sole trader for many years. He decided to change the business status by registering it as a company and selling it to this newly formed entity. The company was incorporated, and Salomon received £39,000 for selling his business to it. Salomon provided a personal loan of £10,000 to the company, backed by a mortgage debenture. When the company encountered financial troubles and went into liquidation, it owed money to both Salomon and other creditors, with only about £6,000 in assets left. Salomon asserted his right as a secured creditor, and the House of Lords upheld his claim, affirming his entitlement to the remaining funds (Marson & Ferris, 2020).

This case highlighted the significance of limited companies by restricting members' liability to their invested shares or money. Proper registration and creditor awareness ensured transparency when trading with a limited company. In other words, when correctly formed and registered (in compliance with statutory requirements), a company possesses its own legal personality, distinct from its members or directors.

We moved on to cover other topics, including:

- **Employment Law**: Understanding rights and obligations in the workplace. These include recruitment and termination. Companies are involved in hiring and firing employees, which implicates employment law. This area focused on: Contract of Employment, Equality in Employment Relationships, Conditions of Employment, Ending Employment Contracts, and Statutory Regulation of Dismissals.

- **Health and Safety**: Employers must oversee worker safety, and situations involving public visits to company premises also fall under legal considerations.

- **Criminal Liability**: Examining legal consequences for criminal acts. It is crucial to understand that civil and criminal liability, although sometimes overlapping, are distinct branches of the law, with separate procedures and purposes. Criminal law aims to regulate actions that violate established laws, defining what is 'against the law' rather than focusing on entitlements. Sanctions and legal consequences serve as deterrents, protect the public, and facilitate rehabilitation. Ultimately, criminal law imposes punishment for illegal acts. In criminal trials, it is the responsibility of the prosecution to prove the defendant's guilt to the extent that there is no reasonable doubt. The accused need not prove their innocence, the responsibility rests with the prosecution. In contrast, civil law plays a vital role in resolving disputes and ensuring that parties uphold their legal obligations. It governs interactions among individuals, businesses, and organisations, covering both voluntary agreements (such as contracts) and situations where society imposes a duty of care (e.g., preventing harm to others). When legal rights are violated, civil law provides mechanisms for remedies. Courts and tribunals handle civil disputes, ensuring fair resolution. Between the two, I grasped the distinction that, unlike criminal cases where the prosecution must prove guilt beyond a reasonable doubt, civil cases are resolved based on the balance of probabilities. In other words, claimants must demonstrate that their version of events is more likely true than not.

Each topic fascinated me, and I embraced the opportunity to learn—which was easy, given my existing interest in law. The impending two-hour exam that would decide our grades, however, was less easy to embrace. Despite the decades that had passed since I last sat an exam (and failed miserably), the format remained the same. The ticking clock, the invigilator's watchful gaze, the tension that hung in the air. The familiar anxiety persisted, bridging past and present. Despite my nervousness, I gave it my all, hoping that my keen interest in the subject had allowed me to absorb all the information that had been laid before us in lectures. I tackled multiple-choice questions and delved into lengthy inquiries on Agency Law, my confidence growing with each question I answered, surprised by the ease at which I did so. In the end, I handed in my completed test paper with a wave of pride, rather than simply relief. I felt content for experiencing an exam, not just the assignments or presentations that had been used to assess my abilities in my previous years. When the results arrived, my combination of passion and hard work had paid off—I achieved a comfortable 75%, earning an A grade in 'Legal Aspect of Business.' This had been my favourite subject to date, and I was even *disappointed* when it was over. No additional law-related modules were included in the degree program, but I felt that my long-standing passion for law, and my keen new interest in business, could easily become intertwined.

In fact, I even considered switching business topics to law and began looking into changing courses. I contemplated speaking to the admissions team to explore the possibility of converting my degree after the second year. However, I realised that my current undergraduate studies are a stroke of luck, and changing to law might not be the best solution. My work in sales and business development aligned with my current studies, and my experience with sales and customer relationships gave me an edge that would contribute to success in a business degree. Given these factors, I believed it was wiser to continue with the business modules, expanding my opportunities for employment in a field that though different, was still stimulating and enjoyable. Law is an exceptional field, and grasping its principles is essential. Even if we're not legal professionals—such as lawyers, barristers, or judges—law profoundly influences our lives. Across all organisations, both in the private and public sectors, adherence to the law is crucial. In the UK, employment law governing employer-employee relationships hold particular significance. Additionally, company law ensures that organisations comply with legal requirements, whether they operate in the UK or elsewhere. I realised that studying law wasn't merely intellectually stimulating, it was vital for me to understand if I were to succeed in business. I had enjoyed revisiting that old passion but also discovered that I was equally as passionate about the new path I was treading.

Outside of business, knowledge of law can open diverse career paths, including accounting, commerce, social work, and even politics. It is important to understand legal regulations in accounting to navigate tax laws. Legal knowledge aids in handling contracts and business regulations. Social workers need to understand family law for child protection and welfare. Lastly, a legal background supports politicians in gaining insights into legislative processes and legal systems. The 'Legal Aspects of Law' module honed reasoning and analytical skills, enabling students to navigate complex situations effectively. Notably, the UK's current Prime Minister, Keir Starmer, obtained a law degree from the University of Leeds, and Sheikh Hasina, former Prime Minister of Bangladesh, was conferred the Degree of Doctor of Law by Boston University, USA (University of Leeds, 2024) (Embassy of Bangladesh, 2020).

Legal knowledge empowers citizens by ensuring they understand their rights and obligations, enabling positive contributions to society. This applies to employers and employees alike, creating a fairer work environment for all. I knew that although this module wasn't going to lead to a job directly connected to law, it would be important information that I would undoubtedly benefit from knowing during my business career.

Sailing through the 'Legal Aspects' module felt like a significant achievement. I had absorbed information that allowed me to ace the first exam I had encountered in decades with confidence, and I felt comfortable knowing that I would be able to navigate the areas where law and business overlapped or clashed. Though the module was over, the door remained open, knowing that this could easily be an avenue I saw myself walking in the future.

Sustainability in Career Development

My experience with the 'Sustainability in Career Development' module was both insightful and rewarding. The module aimed to equip individuals with tools to motivate, develop, and enhance personal growth and career paths. It wasn't just about theoretical concepts - it provided practical guidance. Most of the exercises were conducted through the online career zone at Anglia Ruskin University's Virtual Learning Environment (VLE) and covered a wide range of topics, ensuring that all students could prepare for real-world scenarios.

My assignment involved a concise five-minute online presentation. The topics were personalised - each student, including myself, focused on their desired career profession after completing their degree. I emphasised my interest in pursuing a career in business development as a starting point. I had been inspired by so many topics during my foundation year and first year, with so many unknown elements of business being revealed to me, that it was hard to make a decision. Though I was keenly interested in the legal elements involved in running a business, I'd also been particularly motivated during my 'Business Environment' module. It had sparked daydreams of running my own business and growing something from the ground up, so business development seemed like an appropriate area to delve into. I explored my strengths, my interests, and my occupational values. I considered and researched career achievements and goals and identified opportunities and threats. It was not a decision I made lightly—I had to take stock of my life experiences, my personal skills, and my abilities. In order to choose a path, we must deeply analyse who we are before we can understand who we can be.

I realised that one of my most applicable strengths was my leadership skills. I am the eldest of nine siblings, I am the mother of six children, I had resolved endless conflicts and bickerings and led my family through so many phases in life. Surely, the skills I had developed when managing a large family were something that I could apply to managing a team of people in a business setting. I plunged deeper into myself, identifying more areas in which I had succeeded without even knowing it. Balancing a sometimes chaotic household had given me the gift of adaptability—fulfilling the needs of all of my children, juggling various doctor appointments, or teachers' meetings, or their extra-curricular activities, flowing with their changing demands or sudden requirements.

Surely this is something that would help when managing a business? I had been an interpreter for my abba, which had led me to form strong and fearless communicative skills, and an ingrained understanding of the importance of communication. Was this not a major aspect of national and international business relations? I had needed to be decisive and take action when unforeseen circumstances arose, particularly when I first started my new life here in the UK. I had drive. Commitment. Self-motivation. I was adventurous.

At first, bridging the gap between my personal life and my future as a businesswoman wasn't simple, but I became aware of the many skills that came so naturally to me that I didn't even realise they were there. It wasn't only my home life that showed me my strengths. A particular strength of mine was my sales experience from the various full-time positions I had held since entering the world of work in 2017 after decades of focusing on being a mother and a homemaker. The rapport- building and the development of client relationships that had been part of these work roles were something that I enjoyed and, in fact, excelled at. This had significantly influenced my career aspirations, leading me to set my eyes and ambitions on becoming a Business Development Manager. Though we may not initially realise it, life experiences can be drawn upon as strengths we aren't even aware of, so taking stock of my life in such an in-depth manner gave me a much better understanding of myself.

My efforts bore fruit. My desire to delve into business development as a profession inspired me, and I prepared the assignment presentation with relative ease and absolute eagerness. The presentation required me to explore three questions and answer with insightful answers, which my personal self-assessment made easy.

- **Question 1: Knowing why.** Here, I needed to explain the factors that have shaped my decision to follow business development management as a potential career path. These could include my professional interests, personal strengths, or fundamental values.

My answer:

My strengths: I can establish rapport and relationships with others quickly and easily, I am able to make the right decisions instinctively, show initiative, and I have the ability to bring others around to my way of thinking, winning their agreement.

My interests: I am inquisitive. I like observing, analysing, evaluating, learning, and solving problems. I am enterprising. I am open-minded, good at selling, will do full research before taking action, and seek advantages and opportunities to meet all goals. I am conventional. I am a practical, well-controlled, sociable person who prefers structured tasks.

My occupational values: I am a hard worker and always strive to obtain the best results, hence I like seeing tangible results from work completed. I work extremely hard therefore, I would like income based on productivity. I am a dedicated worker, hence I would like the opportunity for advancement in employment

- **Question 2: Knowing what.** For this, I needed to state which career path I envisioned myself pursuing in the future, focusing, knowing exactly what my career goal was.

My answer:

I would like to become a Business Development Manager. As a business development manager, my strategic role would involve identifying new opportunities for revenue and profitability. I can collaborate with partners, customers, and colleagues, building a wider network. Whether in B2B (business to business) or B2C (business to consumer) contexts, my focus is on growth and connections (Driscoll, 2023). As I gain experience, I can progress to senior positions, overseeing larger teams, and potentially reaching director-level roles (Prospects, 2024).

- **Question 3: Knowing how.** For this question I was required to outline three practical steps I could plan to take that would allow me to enter my future career, ensuring that these goals were achievable given my current and future personal circumstances.

My answer:

- I will complete my degree, which will give me an in-depth knowledge of business.

- I will take an advanced technology course, including the use of Microsoft Excel, in order to abolish this area as a weakness.

- I will start work experience or paid work with training to become a Business Development Manager after graduation.

The soul-searching I had done when starting my assignment had made it quite easy to choose the areas of business I wanted to focus on, but the assignment itself showed me much more. I realised that now I knew what I wanted to do, why I wanted to do it, and how I would set about achieving that goal. My online presentation was duly rewarded with an 'A' grade, reflecting how using my personal experiences as inspiration and motivation had assisted my success. I recognised the significance of self-awareness, goal-setting, and practical application in career development, and knew that I must keep this in mind when faced with future challenges on the topic.

Following obtaining 'A' grades in both the 'Legal Aspects of Business' and 'Sustainability in Career Development' modules, I received an invitation to attend a ceremony for the Top Achiever's Award in Sustainability. Just like that, out of the blue, I was being recognised for my achievements. There are no words to truly convey the feeling. The rush. The sheer, unparalleled joy. In that moment, the way I viewed myself changed. I no longer saw myself as defined as simply a 'mature student.' I was not overlooked as a 'stay-at-home mother of six.' I was Yusra; a person worth recognising, able to be seen. Wherever we are in life, I realised, it is crucial to remain positive, patient, and open-minded.

When faced with failure, remember that something greater might be waiting on the other side. Never lose hope. Instead, keep moving forward on your journey, brushing off what might feel like a defeat in order to make room for success. The moment I received that invitation, my entire outlook shifted. My abba's advice fully made sense - not just wise words, but the unarguable truth. Despite failing my GCSEs twice and temporarily giving up on education, I found alternative paths. I got married at twenty years old, embraced the incredible journey of motherhood, entered the world of work, and then re-entered the world of education. Life had been an amazing roller coaster of ups and downs, twists and turns, chaos and calm, but now I was on a new adventure, and I was accomplishing a whole different kind of recognition.

Managing Human Resources

Though initially seeming straightforward, once we waded deeper into the 'Managing Human Resources' module, it turned out to be particularly challenging. I had been thoroughly enjoying the other modules of this semester, absorbing knowledge and excelling in assignments, blissfully unaware that what felt like a gargantuan challenge was heading my way.

At the start, the class discussions seemed simple - everyone else displayed an understanding of the topic, followed the lessons, and seemed to find the instructions clear. But

I felt like an outsider, looking in, clueless. The complexity of the subject intensified, and so did my anxiety—reaching its peak as the teacher dished out the module assignment report. The report was an in-detail exploration of a variety of points, overlapping and intertwining in a tangle of information. We were required to invent a fictional multinational company based on a real-world counterpart, and align the two based on three critical questions:

- **Recruitment/Selection Process**: How would my fictional company approach recruitment and selection in comparison to the recruitment approach with the existing multinational company?

- **Recruitment Methods**: What strategies would be employed to attract talent for both the imaginary and the real company?

- **Recruitment Interviews**: How would interviews be conducted for both the imaginary and the real company?

Additionally, the report required us to include recommendations for the imagined multinational company we had devised for the project, displaying our initiative when facing the need to hire employees.

I struggled to understand and interpret the assignment's intent. The task of comparing a fictional company with a real-world multinational corporation was intriguing, particularly the concept of building my own fictional company and then analysing it. I wasn't entirely sure what was expected of me, or what the process would teach me. It came to pass that this assignment was designed to allow me to explore my creativity and evolve my analytical prowess, both of which, upon looking at my skills, I felt were particularly weak. But challenges are the stepping stones to growth, so I embraced the challenge, albeit timidly. I pondered the real-world implications, wrestled with concepts, and wondered how to bridge the gap between fiction and reality. By now, success was not just about acing a module - it was about honing my skills, expanding my horizons, and becoming a better version of myself. So, day and night I delved into research, consulted secondary sources, and drew insights from two textbooks – allowing them to be compasses guiding me to understanding: *Introduction to Human Resource Management* by Charles Leatherbarrow and Janet Fletcher (2018) and *Introduction to Human Resource Management* by Paul Banfield, Rebecca Kay, and Dean Royles (2018).

To begin this assignment, I selected the real-life multinational company Bank of Ireland as my reference. Drawing from what I saw, I meticulously crafted an imaginary multinational bank, christening it 'JA Bank.' My analysis delved into recruitment and selection processes, various recruitment methods, and the intricacies of recruitment interviews. By exploring comparisons and contrasts between these two entities, I aimed to unravel insights and uncover unique perspectives. Admittedly, I initially found the process difficult. The distinction between creating an imaginary company and analysing a real one caused uncertainty in my responses, and I was not entirely confident that the recommendations I had developed were quite on target. Nevertheless, I made the best effort with the information at hand. I had to draw on my own resourcefulness to help me navigate the complexities, despite the ambiguity. 'Managing Human Resources' extended beyond the usual coursework, making the path feel unfamiliar.

In addition to the regular coursework, the module included a boardroom meeting assignment with twenty-three practice questions. Participants were expected to show their understanding of the topic in their answers confidently, meaning the research would be an imperative part of preparation. The host emphasised the psychological contract as a key element in the upcoming boardroom practical meeting, so I let my research focus intensely on this subject and discovered the definition of a psychological contract as follows:

According to Hook and Jenkins (2019), the psychological contract differs from a legal contract—it is unwritten, assumed, and unspoken. Although the concept emerged in the 1960s, it gained prominence during the 1990s economic downturn (CIPD, 2012). Chris Argyris (1960) pioneered its application to the workplace, emphasising the expression of employees' needs (Conway & Briner, 2005). Schein (1978) and others further developed this concept (Herriot et al., 1997). The psychological contract reflects the shared understanding of work between employers and employees, encompassing factors like loyalty and expectations of fair treatment. During the boardroom meeting, the host raised a barrage of questions related to this, focusing on employers, employees, and companies.

Here are three similar examples of answers I provided to some of the questions that were posed by the host:

- **The difference between a psychological contract and a legal contract**: as defined by the 'Chartered Institute of Personnel and Development' (CIPD) in 2024, this means that a psychological contract refers to the perceptions that exist within the relationship between employers and workers. While the legal contract of employment provides a limited view of this relationship, the psychological contract goes deeper. It shapes the day-to-day interactions between employers and employees, defining their dynamics. Unlike the tangible legal contract, the psychological contract isn't written down; it's based on how both parties interpret everyday actions. It encompasses expectations, beliefs, and perceived obligations. Essentially, it's the unwritten, assumed, and unspoken understanding between employer and employee. (Hook and Jenkins, 2019).

- **The difference between positive and negative Psychological Contracts and their impact on companies**:

as highlighted by Hook and Jenkins (2019), this outlines that in a positive psychological contract, employees perceive that their contributions to the organisation (such as effort, skills, and commitment) are met with fair rewards and recognition from the employer. When these expectations are effectively managed, it leads to high levels of employee engagement and increased productivity. Balanced and fair exchanges foster a positive employment relationship. Conversely, a negative psychological contract occurs when expectations are not met, leading to feelings of disappointment and let-down among employees. Job satisfaction declines, and employees may experience reduced commitment, performance issues, and turnover intentions. Companies should be cautious, as a negative psychological contract can seriously damage the employment relationship. Understanding and managing psychological contracts are crucial for maintaining positive employee experiences and organisational success.

- **The approaches to flexible working and their impact on positive psychological contracts**: as discussed by Hook and Jenkins (2019), job sharing involves two or more employees dividing the responsibilities of a single role. Employers make arrangements to delegate tasks and responsibilities among the job sharers. This approach fosters collaboration and allows diverse skill sets to work together to achieve a goal. Working from Home (WFH) arrangements allow employees to perform some or all of their work remotely, using modern technology systems and reliable internet services. Some of the advantages encompass less time spent commuting, an improved balance between work and personal life, and greater independence. Zero-hour contracts are prevalent in industries with fluctuating demand or highly seasonal work, but work is unpredictable. In summary, job sharing, working from home and zero-hour contracts, are approaches that can influence positive psychological contracts. Balancing flexibility with stability is crucial for fostering positive relationships between employers and employees.

I dedicated significant time to preparing and revising for the boardroom meeting. However, during the presentation I was faced with difficulty recalling my research. I was sure that I knew the answers, they were there, dashing around in my buzzing brain, but I couldn't quite grasp them. This seemed to have become a pattern for me—perhaps it was part nerves, part failure to memorise the information entirely, but I found myself having to regularly consult my notes for accurate responses with proper references. The examiners required us to cite references for each lengthy question and provide examples in our answers. It was a struggle to memorise all twenty-three, admittedly, but I had no option but to persevere, push myself, and find a way to present the information that I could recall as articulately as possible.

Though I felt immensely out of my depth, my willpower remained, and I was able to land myself a solid 'B' grade. It wasn't the outcome I had hoped for, but it did highlight to me that memorising and recalling a lot of information under pressure was a weaker spot in my skill set and would be something to keep in mind for the next time I may be faced with a similar assignment. This experience reinforced the idea that thinking on my feet and persistence even when uncertain can still yield positive outcomes, and I was determined that I would not let this difficulty get in the way of success.

To me, this felt like both a breakthrough and a barrier, and as the first semester came to a close, I tried not to dwell on the gaping hole I had suddenly become aware of in my skillset. It was time to put learning on pause and replace it with valuable time spent with my family and friends, focusing on something other than education for a while.

The winter break seemed to fly by, and I barely had time to reflect on my eventful first semester before it was suddenly time to steer myself back towards my academic journey.

Semester Two

In mid-January 2023, along with my peers, I welcomed the start of semester two. University doors swung open once more, ushering in new modules for the upcoming term. I had spent the first few weeks of the first semester simply adjusting to the routine of in-person classes, commuting to and from lessons, and navigating the maze of corridors that made up the University of Anglia campus. As we started the second semester, my focus was entirely looking forward, eyes fixed on the path before me. This path was now paved with two new modules, ready to explore— 'Principals and Practice of Marketing' and 'Business Information Systems.'

Principles and Practices of Marketing

The module 'Principles and Practice of Marketing' held a link to my previous experience during the foundation year's 'The Pitch Project,' where I posed as Chief Marketing Officer during a group presentation. It offered a sense of relief, since aspects of marketing weren't entirely unfamiliar. I would be able to draw from what I already knew, rather than starting out without any insight into the topic. In 'The Pitch Project' module, during the foundation year, we explored the 'Four P's' and 'Seven P's' of the marketing mix. The 'Four P's' include product, price, promotion, and place, while the 'Seven P's' expand to include positioning, packaging, and people.

However, in the 'Principles and Practices of Marketing' module, students delved deeper into the 'Seven P's', also known as the 'Seven Tactics in Marketing.' These seven tactics define the market offering, encompassing critical attributes such as product, service, brand, price, incentives, communication, and distribution.

Collectively, these elements shape a company's overall offering. Based on my research and comprehension, the descriptions of each 'Seven Tactics' are as follows:

- **Product** is an item created and sold in large volumes, typically through the manufacturing process. It can be physical (like food, clothing, and furniture) or digital (such as music and software). When customers buy a product, they obtain ownership rights over it. For example, purchasing a car or a software application gives the buyer full ownership of that product (Kotler et al., 2022). A personal example could be the car I use for commuting to work, doing weekly shopping, or visiting relatives. Similarly, a digital software application might be purchased to manage finances or complete university assignments.

- **Service** aims to provide value to customers, but it does not grant ownership rights. Examples of services include appliance repairs, car rentals, medical treatments, and tax filing assistance. The same item can be marketed either as a product or a service. Alternatively, a digital example of this could be a software application that can be sold as a product that gives buyers permanent ownership as mentioned above, or in contrast, provided as a service, enabling users to temporarily lease it and enjoy its features (Kotler et al., 2022). When paying for a service, I might use an appliance repair specialist to fix my broken washing machine, ensuring it runs smoothly without having to buy a new one—an example of using a short-term service to support a product I permanently own. Similarly, I could visit a doctor or a physiotherapist to receive treatment and medical checkups without owning these services but experiencing a long-term benefit.

- **Brand** differentiates a company's products and services from those of its competitors, adding unique value that goes beyond the basic product or service. For example, a luxury car brand distinguishes its vehicles from those produced by other high-end manufacturers. The status of the brand evokes a specific emotional response among customers, who may use it to showcase their wealth and social status (Kotler et al., 2022). Many of us, myself included, will have experienced the desire at some time or another to purchase an item based on the status of the company, displaying the powerful influence successful branding can hold.

- **Price** is the monetary amount exchanged for a particular item or service. It signifies the expense at which something is acquired, enabling customers and partners to enjoy the advantages offered by the company (Kotler et al., 2022).

- **Incentives** are strategies designed to boost the value of an offering by either reducing its costs or enhancing its benefits. These strategies can include volume discounts, rebates, coupons, free gifts, bonus offers, contests, and rewards. They can be aimed at customers, or even the company's partners, like distributors (Kotler et al., 2022). For example, when I do my grocery shopping at a supermarket such as Asda or Tesco, I receive points on my loyalty card that provide discounts on future spending, which encourages me to shop there more frequently. A loyalty card scheme is a strong form of incentive used by many companies, benefitting the customer by providing elements such as discounts or free items, and at the same time benefitting the company or service provider with repeat customers and customer loyalty.

- **Communication** is the process of sharing information between people through a common set of symbols, signs, or behaviours. It includes building personal connections and exchanging verbal or written messages. In a business setting, effective communication ensures that target customers, partners, and stakeholders are informed about the details of a product or service and how to obtain it (Kotler et al., 2022). Communication is a key element of my current role in sales, where I must engage in extended conversations, understand a customer's needs and requirements, build relationships, and effectively communicate what my company has to offer. This effective communication allows me to propose the correct product to customers and make a sale that benefits both the customer and the company.

- **Distribution** refers to the process of sharing or delivering an offering to target customers and company collaborators through specific channels. These channels ensure that products or services reach the intended audience effectively (Kotler et al., 2022). In my previous role as an Account Manager for Coca-Cola, I not only made sales, but also processed orders to ensure customers received their orders on time and correctly. This is part of the distribution channel, without which successful sales would not be fulfilled, to the detriment of the company and customer.

In this module, applying what is known as the 'marketing mix' (marketing tactics) was notably different from my experience as Chief Marketing Officer during the foundation year presentation. The initial task seemed straightforward based on the teacher's briefing, but I discovered its complexity once I delved deeper into the work. For the assignment, I had to choose a company that effectively utilised marketing tactics. I selected Hilton Hotels as my focus company and provided images, along with brief commentaries, on the four marketing tactics (product, price, incentives, and distribution), rather than the full seven tactics. These four tactics highlighted business and marketing strategies related to market segmentation, target marketing, and market positioning. Learning the details of these tactics and the three main areas or marketing in which they are applied gave me an insightful understanding of the way the Hilton Hotel company successfully operates its marketing system. The areas that these tactics are applied to are:

- **Market segmentation**, which refers to the process of dividing a larger consumer group or market into smaller, distinct subsets based on shared characteristics. These subsets may have similar needs, preferences, behaviours, or demographics.

- **Target marketing**, which refers to the specific market segment or group of consumers that a company strategically focuses on to create and capture value.

- **Market positioning**, which describes the strategy a company uses to differentiate its products or services from those of its competitors within a particular market. It involves creating a distinct image or perception in the minds of consumers.

An intriguing aspect of Hilton Hotels is its unique selling point (USP). While many high-end hotel chains offer similar services, Hilton distinguishes itself through a strong dedication to customer satisfaction, exceptional service standardization, and integrated IT systems (Luenendonk, 2019). This offers a good example of how Hilton has considered the marketing mix in order to stand out. Personally, I always prefer to choose Hilton for my holidays. Whenever I walk into a Hilton, the gentle scent of fresh flowers in the lobby welcomes me, setting the tone for a luxurious stay. The plush furnishings and the sophisticated ambiance of the hotel always provide the comfort and elegance that make my holidays truly memorable.

During my assignment, I proposed metrics for evaluating Hilton Hotel's marketing success. However, I felt uncertain about my responses. Instead of addressing market segmentation, target marketing, and market positioning separately, the task required me to combine them into one answer. I naively assumed this would be quite a simple task, but upon further investigation, I realised it was rigorous. I compared it to the business plan and marketing strategies I developed during 'The Pitch Project' in my foundation year, using this as a starting point and drawing from my existing experience. I had to quickly hone the skills that I had started to build during my first exploration into marketing, but despite enjoying my research, I still held some uncertainty about my answers.

I also prepared the group presentation for the 'Principles of Marketing' module. In this presentation, I took on the role of the first person to highlight and present the situation analysis of Premier Inn Hotel. The presentation focused on utilising a PESTLE analysis—a framework that examines external macro-environmental factors affecting organisations or industries. This concept echoed my 'Business Environment' presentation during my first year, where I also employed the PESTLE analysis, so I suddenly felt like I was well within my depth as I set out with this as my starting point. The factors that are focused on when carrying out PESTLE analysis are political, economic, socio-cultural, technological, environmental, and legal aspects. By analysing these factors, businesses gain insights into their external environment, enabling informed decision-making. My thorough studies into the PESTLE analysis factors and their relation to elements of my own sales role gave me an awareness of the impact of each of these factors, detailed as such:

- **Political**: The political environment refers to the system of governance, laws, regulations, and stakeholder dynamics within a country or across supranational bodies. Each country has its own way of governing. For example, China has a different system than the USA or Germany. These systems affect how businesses operate (Needle and Burns, 2019). In my current role at Pierre & Vacances as a Reservation Consultant, I have to be mindful of the different political environments when making hotel bookings in France and Spain, so I was already well versed in learning about the tourism laws, tax regulations, and holidays in these countries, and how they stand as political factors I must consider when conducting bookings. This way, I can ensure that customers from around the world are informed prior to their reservations and are not caught off guard by any factors that may have swayed their decisions or impacted their satisfaction with my services.

- **Economic**: The economic environment encompasses factors like the economic structure (agriculture, mining, manufacturing, and services), economic health (GDP size, growth rates, interest rates, and unemployment levels), and the role of financial institutions (such as banks). Businesses consider these elements when making decisions (Needle and Burns, 2019). This is particularly relatable for me, as in order to be efficient in my role at work, I need to remain well-informed of various economic conditions that would impact my customers' experience. Elements like consumer spending trends, inflation rates, and currency differences between sterling and euros all need to be kept in mind when I make sale, as these trends are subject to fluctuation and can affect the pricing strategies I put forward. Should I fail to be up to date with these details, the information I give to clients would be inaccurate, impacting both my performance and their satisfaction with my services.

- **Socio-cultural**: The socio-cultural environment shapes how businesses operate. The values and beliefs of a society impact business strategies and practices. For example, cultural preferences influence product offerings and marketing approaches. Changes in population demographics matter, considering factors like an ageing population or evolving attitudes toward gender in employment. Analysing the skills of the workforce and their alignment with education is crucial (Needle and Burns, 2019). Not only are major socio-cultural differences, such as cultural norms and social dynamics of various regions, factors that I keep in mind when guiding my clients toward sales. I noticed that language and language barriers are also regular elements that crop up in my work. Understanding different accents and correctly pronouncing things, such as location names, is crucial to my role. If I were to give customers the incorrect pronunciation, it could cause major complications and barriers for them when they come to visit a destination. Likewise, failing to understand a client with a strong accent could result in communication errors on my part. Grasping these socio-cultural nuances is essential for business, especially when trying to make a sale. I often need to adopt different communication strategies for French, Spanish, and Italian speakers, altering the way I speak and listen accordingly. Additionally, my personal history in learning a second language as a child has given me an insight into the intricacies of language and complications caused by language barriers, allowing me to bring my experience from my personal life into my working role.

- **Technological**: Technological factors encompass aspects related to the presence, accessibility, and advancement of technology. These elements significantly influence business operations and strategies like supply chain management systems and automation & robotics (Needle and Burns, 2019). Whilst my background in languages has been a beneficial factor in my sales role, in contrast, my underdeveloped technological skills have been a hinderance at times. I know that my sales performance would be more efficient with more advanced computer literacy, allowing me to more quickly adapt to the use of new booking software or researching competitors' websites. Therefore, it is important to enhance technological skills in business operations to stay competitive, as innovation is primarily driven by technology year after year.

- **Legal**: The legal environment significantly influences companies, shaping their operations and strategies. Some of the aspects include business disputes, business immigration law, and commercial law (Needle and Burns, 2019). This environment is essential for all sectors, whether in business management, other environments, or personal matters. The need for legal services depends on the specific issue at hand. As I learned through my 'Legal Aspects of Business' module, there are numerous legal areas within the legal environment, including business and company law, employment law, educational law, and many more. Failure to remain aware of legal implications of the business environment both here in the UK and within the other countries involved in my sales could have disastrous ramifications. These ramifications could fall upon myself, my customers, or the company I work for, should I make an error. Likewise, the company I work for follows the regulations of its sector as well as implements its own internal regulations, so being thoroughly informed of these details are an integral part of success in my place in the business environment.

- **Environmental**: The environmental factor examines the impacts of ethical and environmental issues in businesses such as fair wages and labour practices, environmental responsibility like waste disposal, and stakeholder treatment such as how companies treat employees, suppliers, and customers (Needle and Burns, 2019). For instance, in my employment, my company prioritises waste and recycling programs, ensuring waste is properly managed, sorted, and disposed of, thereby reducing our environmental footprint. Additionally, my company ensures all safety procedures are adhered to for employee safety, along with providing training programs. This fosters a positive work environment and strengthens relationships between stakeholders.

- In my marketing presentation, which had a strict five-minute time limit, the task involved comparing the UK with another country. I compared the UK with Spain in the context of international business expansion. I focused on Spain's political, economic, socio-cultural, and technological factors. My research covered stability, corporate and income taxes, inflation rates, gross domestic product (GDP) per capita, population, languages, customer behaviour patterns, infrastructure, and smart technology availability. Additionally, recognising cultural nuances is also essential for comprehensive research. In that context, I specifically emphasised the Hofstede Cultural Dimensions when comparing the UK and Spain. These dimensions offer valuable insights into cultural differences and their impact on business practices and management. Taking these cultural aspects into account is essential when planning and launching an international business and failing to do so will likely result in failure. Finally, the presentation concluded by outlining the objectives for opening Premier Inn in Spain as part of its transition from the home market to the international arena. These objectives, spanning the next five years, included establishing three Premier Inn branches in Barcelona, Valencia, and Seville, Spain.

Immediately following my group presentation, we were informed that points would be deducted for reading from notes during the presentation, including my own. This was another blow for me, and I was frustrated with myself. I had once again relied on my notes when discussing the multifaceted factors related to Spain—covering political, economic, social, and technological aspects. The prospect of memorising extensive content, complete with numerical figures, for each topic felt daunting, and I felt much more comfortable keeping references to hand to ensure that I was relaying accurate information. Though the presentation was only five minutes long, it required that I highlight many facts and figures, which I had not been able to do entirely from memory. My life was increasingly busy, with strains on my time already coming from full-time work and caring for a large family, so finding a way to cram all of this information into my brain was challenging, and unfortunately, was a challenge I had not yet overcome. I also realised that the anxiety surrounding my stammer had been creeping in, causing me to spill my words out like water from a dam that had been broken. Though I had done well up until this point to control my anxiety around speaking, the strict five-minute time limit that had been placed upon us had unravelled me a little. Revising and practising is one thing, but when the pressure is on, things very quickly become very different.

Despite these obstacles, I achieved a 'B' grade in 'Principles of Marketing.' I knew I would have to take this as the push I needed in order to work on improving this part of myself. I evidently had not been able to rectify my need to rely on notes, since it had previously impacted my success in other modules, and this was the final straw. The ability to relay important information when called upon would be imperative for success, so I vowed to maintain a positive mindset and harness resilience, making sure that this would never be my downfall again. Though a 'B' grade is something to be proud of, I had hoped for more. But even if the results aren't exactly what you hoped for, the satisfaction of trying and refusing to give up is invaluable.

Business Information Systems

At the same time, I was also dealing with the module called 'Business Information Systems.' This topic revolves around technology and modern systems used to manage information within organisations. It encompasses various aspects related to business information systems, including hardware, software, databases, networks, and functional applications. I still had very limited knowledge of technology, having had next to no technological skills when I first embarked on my course. My comfort zone only extended to basic tasks like turning on a computer, checking emails, and performing simple Google searches. When it came to more complex concepts related to modern technology, I felt overwhelmed. 'Business Information Systems' focuses on the tools, software, and hardware used to manage information within a business. It encompasses databases, enterprise resource planning (ERP) systems, customer relationship management (CRM) software, and more. To enhance my preparation for this module, I utilised secondary research materials to enhance my content. Notably, I referenced the textbook titled *Business Information Systems: Technology, Development, and Management for the Modern Business* (sixth edition) by Paul Bosij, Andrew Greasley, and Simon Hickie. This book provided me with comprehensive knowledge and understanding of Business Information Systems terminology and offered valuable guidance, which helped me complete my presentation and assignments successfully.

The themes related to information systems are:

- **Hardware & Software**: Understanding the components of computer systems (hardware) and the programs that run on them (software).

- **Database & Analytics**: Learning about databases, data modelling, and how to extract meaningful insights from data.

- **Networks**: Exploring how information flows across networks, including local area networks (LANs) and wide area networks (WANs).

- **Enterprise and Functional Systems**: Studying systems that support specific business functions (e.g., finance, human resources, supply chain) and how they integrate into the overall enterprise.

- **Customer Relationship Management (CRM)**: Exploring how systems bridge the gap between Enterprise Resource Planning (ERP) systems and customers. They encompass the entire process of establishing and maintaining customer relationships. CRM systems are designed to integrate various information systems containing customer-related data. These systems include databases with customer details and preferences, sales order processing applications, and Salesforce automation tools. The overarching goal is to acquire and retain customers while enhancing their engagement with the organisation.

- **Salesforce**: A computer program that helps companies manage their relationships with customers. It allows businesses to find potential customers, close deals, and provide good service after the sale. Salesforce automation involves streamlining the entire sales cycle, from lead generation to closing a sale and providing after-sales service, using Customer Relationship Management (CRM) systems (Bocij et al., 2018).

While I knew my limited computer literacy would be a hindrance, I hoped to build upon it as I progressed in my studies. My goal was to gradually explore the complexities of business information systems and deepen my understanding. Since 2017, in my various roles at my current organization, I had been using Salesforce and CRM systems to manage business account holders' accounts. This involved studying them to determine the conversations I should initiate, the questions I should ask, and my objectives after identifying the services they have already used. Salesforce and CRM have helped me establish and maintain customer relationships and conduct sales calls from start to finish.

I found myself in a pivotal situation when I was unexpectedly assigned the role of Chief Technology Officer (CTO) for a group presentation. The news caught me off guard, and I was rattled by how out of my league I felt. It was a daunting responsibility—one I wasn't prepared for. As a team member, I recognised that everyone had their roles, but I grappled with uncertainty about how to fulfil my CTO responsibilities. I didn't know where to begin, and panic started to seep in, so I decided it would be best to reach out to the module teacher. I explained my situation to the teacher, emphasising my lack of expertise in technology. It was a point of embarrassment that, in this day and age, I was so unfamiliar with technology, but I had simply had no need to utilise it beyond the basics until now. To my relief, the teacher listened attentively and responded with empathy. He assured me that he would be happy to offer assistance throughout the presentation. He would guide me step by step, helping me understand how to begin, what content was necessary, and which topics I should cover. I knew that this knowledge would not come to me overnight, but the teacher's support eased my anxiety.

I forced myself to face this challenge head-on, drawing inspiration from my abba's wisdom: "After hardship, light will shine." The memory of abba's resilience encouraged me to tackle the role with determination. Despite the unknown territory, language barriers, and uncertainty he had faced when he moved his family over 5,000 miles to start a new, better life in the UK, he had taken on the changes and challenges that came with it and had found ways to navigate life here. I had always admired this about him. Despite everything being so alien and unfamiliar to abba, he had learned and adapted. Technology was alien and unfamiliar to me, so it was time for me to mirror him. I decided to move forward, taking one step at a time, rather than letting cowardice or foolishness lead me to continue avoiding the difficulties that stood in my way. My bold childhood spirit still resided, deep within me. It had once made me fearless during my school days, and now I reclaimed it, using it to empower me as I tackled my degree modules. Giving up was not an option.

I reflected on my own journey—raising six children day by day, year after year. You can read every parenting book on the shelf, but without passion, willpower, and strength, you will still be unprepared to tackle such a significant responsibility. I had somehow managed to do this six times over, so surely those qualities were in me. Armed with this self-awareness, I resolved to put in the unwavering effort to tackle the CTO role that had been bestowed upon me, and to conquer any of the obstacles that would come with it. I was reaching into the unknown, preparing myself with information and support from my teacher. Without drive, I knew I could not succeed. This knowledge alone was enough to grant me said drive.

My group decided to base their presentation on Uber, the taxi service. The module teacher guided me through the necessary research into the company that would be needed and helped to outline my role and responsibilities. My task was to create a visual representation of Uber's journey using symbols and images, rather than only using text. This journey would encompass everything, from the initial passenger request to the drop-off, utilising various technological devices and incorporating modern world systems, including artificial intelligence. Though a little baffled by the concept, I was undeterred by the challenge and set about crafting a detailed diagram. I meticulously depicted Uber's journey, using Google Maps images to illustrate the functionality at each stage. Despite having seen the process demonstrated only once by the teacher, I went the extra mile, not only recreating every element as I had been shown but also practising and perfecting the technique. It took time, and I had to make a few attempts, but it was my responsibility to do so.

My hard work paid off and my teacher was impressed by the completed diagram, particularly since I had come from a total lack of prior experience. He praised me for my efforts, understanding, and outstanding outcome. Without the teacher's guidance, I recognised that comprehension would have been elusive. My success was also his success. This principle holds true not only in academic settings but also in various aspects of life.

Whether it's a presentation, a project, or a challenge, clarity about the task at hand is fundamental. By seeking support and grasping the context, we can navigate challenges effectively and achieve our goals.

On the day of the presentation, I faced a different kind of challenge—it was the very first day of Ramadan (a month of fasting for Muslims, abstaining from food and drink between sunrise and sunset), and I was fasting. I was at times distracted by my hunger, but despite this, practise continued throughout the day, preparing myself and my team to perform the presentation at 6 pm. To my absolute joy (and a level of surprise), I managed to convey all the relevant information within the tight time frame of four minutes. Our presentation ran seamlessly, and we excelled in the assignment. My thorough approach and commitment to excellence were evident, earning me praise from both my team and the audience, including the teacher, making the worries I had grappled with at the start of the assignment feel so far away I could hardly remember them.

Figure 4: Business Information Presentation of the CTO, March 2023

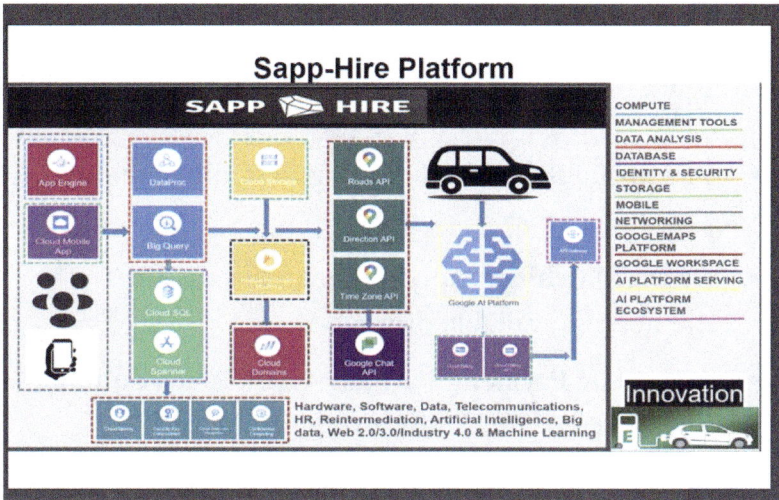

Source: Created by Yusra Mariyam

Figure 4 shows my 'Business Information Systems' presentation diagram, where I carried the role of Chief Technology Officer (CTO) in the fictional Sapp-Hire Taxi Company, inspired by Uber. The diagram utilises Google Cloud Services, which is a specifically developed suite of eleven different software programs often used by businesses in their day-to-day running, with each element serving a different purpose. The Google Cloud Services include Compute, Management Tools, Data Analysis, Database, Identity & Security, Storage, Mobile, Networking, Google Maps Platform, Google Workspace, and Artificial Intelligence (AI) Platform Serving. The diagram explores how these services are managed within the five steps behind Sapp-Hire bookings:

- **Customer Request:** Passengers use smartphones to request a ride via the app, specifying their destination and viewing the fare estimate.
- **Pickup Confirmation:** Passengers confirm their pickup location.
- **Driver Matching:** Sapp-Hire matches the ride with the nearest available driver.
- **Automatic Payment:** Payment is processed automatically via credit or debit cards after the ride.
- **Rating System:** Both passengers and drivers rate each other (Singh, 2024).

To summarise, the entire process shown in my diagram—from customer requests, through the completion of rides and the rating system—is depicted using Google Cloud Products. Each row in the diagram corresponds to a specific service within the Google Cloud ecosystem.

- Row one is the request of the customer using a smartphone.
- Row two shows a managed data warehouse that helps to manage built-in features like machine learning, which predicts future events based on historical data like ratings received from customers. The second row also consists of cloud products and prevents issues

such as identity-based attacks, data breaches, and security.

- Row three is the cloud storage for keeping and accessing data, fireball performance monitoring that helps the performance of the Apple and Android apps, and cloud domains that register, manage, and transfer existing domains.

- Row four is Google Maps, which helps with directions, roads and places on mobile apps. Additionally, Google Chat API is similar to Industry 4.0, which helps to integrate between the drivers and customers as big data is managed between humans and machines.

- Row five demonstrates the Sapp-Hire booking, and the driver leading the ride with the customer. The Google artificial intelligence platform, which is the modern technologies using the internet of things, the big data, and the Web 2.0 and Web 3.0. These are digital network platforms spanning all connected devices. They also include customer payment methods with the Cloud billing towards the end of the journey.

- Row 6 shows the API gateway of the diagram, which enables the provision of secure access to the back-end services.

The presentation was not the end of 'Business Information Systems.' There was another assignment—to write about what is known as 'blockchain.' I learned that Blockchain acts as an unalterable digital record, ensuring secure transactions across a network. It records, stores, and verifies data without the need for banks or governments. Each transaction is captured in a block, forming a continuous chain of connected data.

Our tutor told us to think of it as a tamper-proof digital train where each carriage (block) holds data, and passengers (transactions) travel securely from one station to the next. Beyond its association with cryptocurrencies like Bitcoin, blockchain technology finds broader applications across various industries. Bitcoin is essentially virtual coins moving across the internet—no physical notes or coins are needed. You can buy, trade, and use it to purchase goods. Unlike traditional money overseen by banks or governments, Bitcoin relies on a global network of computers using blockchain technology (Bocij et al., 2018). I might have heard the terms 'Blockchain' or 'Bitcoin' before, but it was through this module that I truly understood their meanings.

The remained written assignment about blockchain had three points to address:

- I needed to identify and assess the key characteristics and global importance of blockchain, focusing on its essential features and worldwide impact.

- I needed to examine the opportunities and challenges that blockchain presents to my chosen sector. Specifically, I analysed how blockchain affects opportunities and challenges within the transport industry.

- I had to apply Porter's value chain and/or Rayport & Sviolka's virtual value chain to examine how blockchain generates and delivers value in our business. This analysis was specifically aimed at understanding how blockchain enhances value for Sapp-Hire, the fictional company I created for my presentation.

My experience with my 'Business Information Systems' assignment highlights an important lesson—confidence alone isn't enough. Let's break down my situation: I felt more comfortable with understanding and completing the written work than with maths or technology, so I approached the assignment confidently. However, when it came to the written assignment with this module, I underestimated it and didn't seek extra guidance from the teacher. Instead, I relied on basic secondary research, completed the assignment, and submitted it by the deadline.

The outcome was good: I scored 70% (an 'A' grade) for my CTO presentation. My confidence stemmed from thorough preparation, understanding the material, and delivering a strong presentation once I grasped the teacher's instructions, hence confidence can be a great asset when backed by knowledge and correct preparation. However, I obtained a 'C' grade for the written assignment. This is because my prior success had made me overconfident, tricking me into thinking I knew where I was heading without even checking. Overconfidence can lead to weaker results, as when we assume we know everything, we may miss crucial details or fail to explore deeper insights. Despite this mix of results, my overall 'B' grade in 'Business Information Systems' reflects commitment and adaptability. But it also serves as a reminder—balancing confidence with humility, acknowledging our limitations and seeking help when needed, can lead to far better outcomes.

Throughout my second year, I demonstrated a mix of growing confidence, important lessons learned, and tenacity. Despite setbacks, I became committed to bettering myself and my skills, embracing new information and identifying weaknesses that I had previously been unaware of. I had excelled confidently in 'Legal Aspect of Business' and 'Sustainability in Career Development' with 'A' grades, but I faced challenges in the remaining three modules. I had a lot to learn, but I didn't shy away from these difficult phases. Instead, I persevered, seeking solutions and learning from my mistakes. I achieved a confident, higher, 'B' grade across those three modules, with which I was quite happy. After all, the process had been turbulent but had been far more rewarding than receiving top marks.

By the end of April 2023, all modules and examinations of year two had been completed, graded and reviewed. My second year had been significantly more challenging than those that had come before it, and despite the enjoyment I was getting from learning, I will admit that I was welcoming the upcoming summer break. I needed to reflect on all that I had learned about my modules, about business, and about myself. Face-to-face classes had been demanding and had forced me to embrace a new type of learning. I had seen gaps in my learning style that I had not previously been aware of, and the light that had been shone on them would allow me to become a better student and ultimately, a better businesswoman. The relief of the summer break was palpable, and I eagerly planned a two-week holiday to unwind and reward myself. As much as hard work is needed to succeed, relaxation and self-care are needed to do the hard work in the first place, so I relished the vacation. I knew that before long, my summer would be over, and I would once again have to replace downtime with studies, as my third year beckoned on the horizon.

Reflecting on my second year of university, to me, it unfolded like a captivating story—a tapestry woven with diverse modules, unforeseen challenges, and personal triumphs. I appreciated the summer break, but anticipation bubbled within me as I eagerly awaited the next instalment—the grand finale of my academic journey. My resilience, determination and willingness to learn allowed me to navigate the twisting corridors and pathways I had encountered during the learning process. It had taken some time and a few knocks, but the qualities I had possessed as a youngster were returning, and I had seen them gradually but surely blossoming within me once more over the three years of my studies so far. However, resilience is not just a requirement within the halls of academia, it's a life skill—an armour we must wear to face the world's uncertainties. In the face of adversity, I found solace in alternative strategies and creative problem-solving. When the tempests raged, I remained anchored, knowing that tough days are transient visitors— they don't set up permanent residence. A positive outcome always waits on the horizon, obscured by the clouds of challenge, but there, nonetheless.

Balancing the scales, I weighed my difficult phases against possible solutions, seeking equilibrium. *What can I change? How can I transform negativity into opportunity? How can I twist each hardship to become beneficial?* These questions propelled me forward, like a ship navigating treacherous waters. Success isn't handed out like candy - it's forged in the crucible of hardship. We defy the odds, not because it's easy, but because it's necessary. The impossible becomes merely a challenge—a gauntlet thrown down by fate. With resilience as our compass, we navigate uncharted territories, discovering hidden strengths and unimagined possibilities. We must wield our inner strength like a sword, our determination as our shield, ready to take on the tribulations that we will undoubtedly face. Within the unknown, lies the greatest adventure, and as I teetered on the edge of my final year as a student, I was ready to take the plunge.

Chapter References

Banfield, P., Kay, R. and Royles, D. (2018). *Introduction to Human Resource Management.* Oxford University Press.

Bocij, P., Greasley, A. and Hickie, S. (2018). *Business Information Systems,* 6th edition. Pearson Publishing.

CIPD (2012). Where has all the trust gone?

CIPD (2024). Psychological contract.

Conway, N. and Briner, R.B. (2005a) *The history and development of the psychological contract concept | understanding psychological contracts at work: A critical evaluation of theory and research | oxford academic.*

Driscoll, D. (January 2023), *Business development manager.* University Compare. https://universitycompare.com/guides/career/business-development-manager.

Embassy of Bangladesh. (2020.) *Sheikh Hasina – honourable prime minister, government of the People's Republic of Bangladesh.* Embassy of Bangladesh. https://bangladeshembassy.nl/honourable-prime-minister-detail/.

Herriot, P., Manning, W.E.G. and Kidd, J.M. (1997). The content of the psychological contract. *British Journal of Management.* Wiley Online Library.

Hook, C. and Jenkins, A.K. (2019). *Introducing Human Resource Management.* Pearson Education, Ltd.

Kotler, P., Keller, K.L. and Chernev, A. (2022). *Marketing Management,* 16th edition. Marketing Management.

Leatherbarrow, C. and Fletcher, J. (2024). *Introduction to Human Resource Management.* Kogan Page.

Luenendonk, M. (September 2019). *Business model of Hilton hotels.* Cleverism. *https://www.cleverism.com/business-model-hilton-hotels/.*

Marson, J. and Ferris, K. (2020). *Business Law.* Oxford University Press.

Needle, D. and Burns, J. (2019). *Business in Context: An Introduction to Business and its Environment,* 7th edition. Cengage Learning EMEA.

AGCAS editors. (May 2024) *Business development manager job profile.*

Prospects. https://www.prospects.ac.uk/job-profiles/business-development-manager.

Singh, M. (2024). How to build an app like Uber. *FATbit Blog. University of Leeds (2024) University alum becomes UK prime minister, University of Leeds.*

Chapter Five:

Final Year

In the summer of July 2023, I decided that it was time to make a life-changing leap. The tribulations of the presentation projects in the second year of my degree highlighted to me that despite a lifetime of trying to control my stammering during nerve-wracking moments, I had never actually sought effective support. As I prepared for my final year of university, I was forced to reflect on the impact that my stammer had on my success during class discussions and presentations. I knew that the coming year would bring more modules that would no doubt be laced with assignments requiring me to speak to an audience, and this gave me great anxiety.

The idea of seeking help for something that I had felt so personally ashamed of for so long haunted me, but after long, deep contemplation, I finally found the courage to take the first steps in breaking these shackles. I decided to consult a speech therapist who specialised in stammering, explaining that my difficulties in controlling my stammer during gatherings, interviews and presentations had been holding me back. It felt like my own tongue was standing between myself and my full potential in these scenarios. Before venturing out into the world of work, I had rarely found myself in situations that required me to speak publicly, and the coping mechanisms I had developed over my life were not enough to see me through the more high- pressure conditions I was now encountering. Yes, my communication skills had becoming strong when helping my parents as a translator, but this was a very different type of communication than translating the information in my head to the words coming out of my mouth under pressure.

Over five consecutive sessions with the speech therapist, I learned techniques for handling my stammer and practised slowing down my speech. The stammering consultant taught me to observe how Barack Obama (former president of the USA) speaks, emphasising the importance of taking time and speaking slowly and clearly. He also advised me to read paragraphs aloud, record myself, and then watch the recordings, helping me to become aware of my speech patterns and understand what other people heard when I spoke. I was able to identify areas for improvement and monitor my progress, paying attention to pacing myself and holding back the words as they tried to stumble out of my mouth chaotically or without clarity. In each session, I saw a difference in my communication, realising that it had taken a little guidance, self-awareness and determined practice to set me on the right path, reversing the life-long block that had stood between myself and my voice.

As my sessions with the speech therapist came to an end, I realised the profound difference that the simple act of reaching out for help would now have on my life. I was even a little frustrated at myself that I hadn't considered this earlier in life. Abba had always taught me that what I have to say is of value, but I had never quite gotten the hang of simply how to say it. I felt content. I had acknowledged what I had always seen as a flaw and taken steps to overcome the difficulties that came with it, rather than trying to simply sweep it under the rug and hide it. It wasn't until I began my university studies that I finally understood the value of reaching out for help, even though it required exposing a weakness, and that letting go of the fear of asking for assistance is much braver than struggling alone.

Life's challenges can often provide the push we need, the urge to go one step further to make that change, but it takes courage and vulnerability to do so. One of the biggest lessons that I had learned was that to delay seeking assistance was to delay seeking success.

As the summer rolled to a peaceful end, so did the freedom that came with it. I was soon to find my long walks and cherished spare time to be replaced with the structured routine and endless hours of studying that came with life as a mature student. It felt like entering a metaphorical 'jail' that I would have to stay caged in until the semester ended. It wasn't that I didn't enjoy my university course, I knew that the rewards for completing my degree would far outweigh the sacrifices made to achieve it, but each academic year it had taken time for me to readjust to the new routine.

I was already balancing a full-time job and caring for my brimming household, so attending university for two evenings and a Saturday every week, as well as further studying and completing assignments in every spare hour I had, was a strain. However, I knew that the 'jail' was only in my mind and that the constraints on my time were only temporary. I only had one year left to serve in my 'jail,' then I would be free to soar higher and further than I could have imagined four years previously. Besides, there was a silver lining to these struggles—I had been finding great joy in excelling in each year of my degree and progressing significantly. I noticed that I had learned as much about myself as I had about business, and these achievements far outweighed any difficulties I was having about these impermanent sacrifices.

As always, the days leading up to the start of studies danced with the familiar questions: *What would the new modules be like? Who would my new tutor be? Could I handle what this final year was about to throw my way?* These questions had been echoing with each new year of my studies, they had become familiar foes, but each year they grew weaker. I was also fizzing with excitement—an eager anticipation to reunite with classmates, especially those who had now become close friends. Just like the rest of the nation, the crushing impact that COVID-19 had on my social life had left me feeling isolated, so this new group of diverse but like-minded people that had been brought into my life thanks to my in-person classes had been welcomed—another unexpected gift from becoming a student. The classroom awaited, and when I stood at the threshold of challenge, I assisted by camaraderie.

This kind of social integration and acceptance had not always been easy for me. I come from an Asian and Muslim background and typically dress according to my culture and religion, which hasn't always been accepted with open arms. When I began my ventures into full-time work, I also began to adapt my outfits to balance my religious beliefs with modern professional norms in the UK. I came to understand that this balancing act is essential for harmonious living. In a business setting as well as a social setting, first impressions count, and learning how to integrate myself into those settings was key. As a child, though I had at times been aware of my 'otherness,' I had still fit in with my peers relatively easily. Of course, as with many Muslim people, there were times when I had been very aware that my presence was not entirely met without friction from some individuals, but I had always held my head high and carried on. Over the years, as I failed two sets of GCSE exams and saw two dream careers slip out of reach, my self-assurance took a hit. Following that, my two and a half decades of being a homemaker and mother of six saw me spending most of my time surrounded by my own culture, so when it came to stepping out into the world of work in 2017, part of the adventure was learning how to bridge the gap between my heritage and my new environment.

Striving for equilibrium—whether in fashion choices or other aspects of life—can lead to a fulfilling and authentic existence. However, it's important to remember our roots, no matter how much we try to fit in. Valuing my roots, culture and religion, whilst also adapting to different environments, making new friends, and managing life with peers and colleagues from all over the world was daunting at first, but embracing diversity is not as hard as people often believe. Though at first, this had felt alien, just as it did when I first moved to the UK as a wide-eyed child, I began to realise that it is not *me* who is different. We are *all* different. By respecting and celebrating diversity, I could also be accepted for who I am.

Forgetting my identity would mean losing myself, and compromising my values wouldn't earn me respect. Learning to combine my culture with a business environment was assisted by these understandings, so I did not see the slight alteration of my wardrobe as a deviation from my roots, but part of the birth of my true identity—'Yusra, The Businesswoman.' British, Bangladeshi, and bold. I strive to advocate for anyone to understand that they deserve equal opportunities, and that they can achieve this without forgetting the value of one's roots. After all, to receive love, you must first love yourself. To receive respect, you must first respect yourself. And to be valued, you must first value yourself, your identity, and your heritage.

Semester One

Gearing up for the long-awaited September Saturday, the start of my final year, felt much more daunting than I had expected. I hoped I was ready, having worked so hard to get this far, but I still felt as though there was something missing. I fondly recalled my abba, imagining his firm hand on my shoulder, his eyes dancing with pride. I found myself wishing so deeply that he was there with me, sharing every struggle, triumph, and excellent grade from my previous years of study. I longed to hear his encouragement as I stood at the starting line of the journey to the end of my degree. His joy and pride would have been immeasurable. Despite my heavy heart, *Abba's* words still echoed in my mind: "Keep going, and results will manifest one day." And so, I found myself once more pushing at the heavy door that stood between myself and my business career, having pushed for three years and seen it inch open a little more each day. I knew that the pushing was almost over, that in just seven months that door would finally swing open, revealing the light on the other side, just as abba had always promised it would.

This realisation was also bittersweet. Though there was a sense of relief that this final year was the last leg of what felt like a marathon, when this academic year concluded, university life would come to an end. The familiar routine of attending lessons, making notes, burying myself in books, and seeing classmates would fade away, replaced with—hopefully—a brand new adventure, and a thriving career in business. Of course, this also came with the anticipation of my final grade, determining whether I would even graduate at all, and if so, at what level: third-class, lower-second-class, upper-second-class, or first-class honours. Though the pressure was immense, I'd worked diligently semester by semester, year after year, and I refused to let it slip away now. It was time to dedicate myself beyond one hundred per cent, if there were such a thing.

My identity was evolving. I was still Yusra—a girl who arrived in the UK at the age of seven, powered through language school, and quickly became proficient in English, excelled in swimming at eight years old, and thrived in my earlier years in the British education system. And yes, it seemed as though things hit a wall from there, and that life spun me in an unexpected direction, but now I stood tall, as a mature student, aiming to prove that my daring spirit had been rekindled, and aspiring to conquer what I had once thought the impossible. I reminded myself that, though the end was the destination, I needed to keep my eyes fixed on the road. I would have to meticulously face every assignment and let nothing go over my head, no grade slip through my fingers. I knew where the finish line lay, there on the stage, graduating with glowing grades, but I would need to focus on the path to avoid tripping along the way. With that, I was ready to roll. My first semester would consist of two modules: 'Managing Business Operations,' and 'Executing Business Strategy.' I was mildly dubious - my knowledge of what to expect from these topics was limited, and my existing understanding was vague, but it was time to stride back into the classroom and find out.

Managing Business Operations

The familiar faces of my classmates were a welcoming sight—each one filled with curiosity, smiles, and the enjoyment of reconnecting. Everyone was present and correct, equally as keen as I was to get this final year started, when we were met with a new face: the module's teacher. Though new to me, I could quite quickly tell that this was a person I could trust to guide me as I ventured forth. Positioned at the front of the classroom near his desk, he introduced himself and greeted all the students, taking time to ask for introductions from each of us in return. When all ears were intently focused on his words, he began to explain the upcoming module.

This first module of the semester—'Managing Business Operations'—aimed to explain the role of an 'Operations Manager' within a company, as well as the responsibilities involved with this position. I was not unfamiliar with the term, having encountered several managers in my professional life who held the job title, but I was not aware of exactly what these colleagues did within the company. In the initial two sessions of this module, the module teacher uncovered the ins and outs of the role. Our tutor explained in depth that business operations management is the discipline that focuses on how organisations create and deliver services and products. It covers everything from the clothes you wear and the food you eat to the furniture you sit on, the devices you use, the books you borrow, the medical treatments you receive, the services you expect in shops, and the lectures you attend at university. Operations managers are behind all these experiences, meticulously organizing the creation and delivery of these goods and services. While they may not always carry the title 'Operations Manager,' their role is pivotal (Slack & Brandon-Jones, 2019).

I delved deeper into operations management, which centres on managing business practices to achieve peak efficiency within an organisation. In manufacturing firms, this involves efficiently transforming materials and labour into goods and services to maximise profits. Essentially, business operations management comes with the responsibility of optimising resources and processes to efficiently achieve organisational goals. This role requires the employee to consider the input of resources such as materials, information, technology, employees, and customers needed within a company. These resources are then transformed into outputs, such as customers acquiring products or services. This successful operation adds value for customers, generates sales, and contributes to the company's overall profit (Slack & Brandon-Jones, 2019). The operations function plays a central role in any organisation because it is accountable for creating and delivering all goods and services—the very reason for the organisation's existence. I learned that there are three main functions within an organisation:

- **Marketing**, which includes sales, is responsible for promoting the organization's offerings to its target markets, with the goal of generating customer demand.

- **Product/Service Development**: This role involves designing new and improved services and products while also predicting future customer needs.

- **Operations:** This role is dedicated to producing and delivering services and products according to customer demands. It ensures that processes are efficient, and resources are used effectively.

In addition, 'Managing Business Operations' covers essential topics such as process types, layouts, supply chain management, lean operations, total quality management, and project management.

Diving into this module seemed never-ending, with countless topics to explore and expand my knowledge. It proved to be more intricate than I first thought, and I even felt that I have underappreciated the hard work that goes into managing business operations. We next looked into more detailed breakdowns of the topics, as follows:

- **Process Types**: The placement of a process on the volume–variety spectrum affects its design and the method of managing its activities. These methods are referred to as process types. The terminology for these types can differ depending on whether they are mainly manufacturing or service processes, with some overlap in terms. For example, manufacturing terms are occasionally applied in service industries (Slack & Brandon-Jones, 2019).

The manufacturing process types are:

- **Project processes:** involve producing unique, often highly customized products, usually with considerable time intervals between completions. Each project has a defined start and finish, marked by low volume but high variety. The activities within these processes can be ambiguous and uncertain, requiring resources to be specially organised for each distinct item. The complexity of these processes often stems from the need for professional judgment and discretion. Examples of these processes include developing software, producing films, undertaking most construction projects, and conducting large-scale fabrication operations such as manufacturing turbo generators (Slack & Brandon-Jones, 2019). Other examples of project processes in different industries include event planning, such as organizing conferences, weddings, concerts, and corporate meetings, which require detailed planning, coordination, and execution. Urban planning also necessitates complex planning with various stakeholders. Aircraft manufacturing involves intricate designing, assembling, and testing processes.

- **Jobbing Processes**: these handle high variety and low volumes, with products sharing resources. Each item requires similar attention but has unique needs. Examples include custom tailoring, precision toolmaking, furniture restoration, and printing event tickets (Slack & Brandon-Jones, 2019). Additional examples include handcrafted pottery, producing unique pottery items that cater to specific design requests, and tailored clothing, where custom clothing items are designed and sewn based on individual measurements and preferences.

- **Batch processes**: these are similar to jobbing processes but with less variety. They produce multiple items at once, repeating each stage during production. Small batches resemble jobbing, while larger, familiar batches become repetitive. These processes span various volume and variety levels. Examples include machine tool manufacturing, gourmet frozen food production, and making components for mass-produced items like cars (Slack & Brandon-Jones, 2019). Additional examples include pharmaceutical manufacturing, which produces batches of medications such as tablets or capsules that run through different stages of formulation, mixing, and packaging. Another example is cosmetic production, where skincare or makeup products undergo similar processes.

- **Continuous processes**: these make large quantities of items with little variety, running for long periods without stopping. They use expensive, specialised equipment, and operate in a very predictable way. The main feature is the smooth flow from one stage to the next. Examples include water treatment, refining oil, generating electricity, making steel, and producing certain types of paper. (Slack & Brandon- Jones, 2019). Additional examples include glass manufacturing, which involves continuous melting, forming, and heat treatment processes, and cement production, which includes grinding, heating, and cooling stages.

- **Mass processes**: these involve producing items in large quantities with limited variety. Although there may be many variants, the core production process remains unchanged. These processes are usually repetitive and predictable. Examples include automatic packing lines, car assembly plants, and TV manufacturing (Slack & Brandon-Jones, 2019). Another example is bottling plants for water, soft drinks, and juices, which involve filling, capping, and labelling bottles in a highly automated and repetitive manner.

After learning about the different manufacturing process types, I became aware that knowing their characteristics and benefits is crucial for making informed decisions. This insight helps enhance production efficiency, lower costs, and improve product quality, which is essential for anyone in manufacturing or production planning. Below are the service process types:

- **Professional services**: are characterised by high levels of customer interaction, where clients are deeply involved in the service process. These services are highly customisable, tailored to meet the specific needs of each customer. Generally, professional services focus more on people than on equipment, with employees having significant autonomy in how they deliver services. Examples include management consulting, legal practices, architecture, medical clinics, auditing, health and safety inspections, and some computer field service operations (Slack & Brandon-Jones, 2019). Additional examples include educational consulting, which offers advice and strategies for seeking academic improvement, and human resources consulting, which delivers bespoke HR solutions including recruitment, talent management, and organizational development.

- **Service shops**: function with a balanced mix of volume, variety, customer interaction, customisation, and staff autonomy, positioning them between professional and mass services. They provide services through a blend of front-office and back-office operations. Examples include banks, retail stores, holiday tour operators, car rental agencies, schools, most restaurants, hotels, and travel agencies (Slack & Brandon-Jones, 2019). Additional examples include beauty salons and spas, which provide a range of beauty and wellness treatments, mixing scheduled appointments with walk-in services. Another example is cafes and coffee shops, where both dine-in and take-out options are available.

- **Mass services**: these handle numerous customer transactions with minimal contact time and limited customisation. Staff typically have clearly defined roles and follow specific procedures. Mass services include supermarkets, national rail systems, airports, telecommunications providers, libraries, TV stations, police departments, and utility customer service desks. Call centres are a common example, managing large volumes of customer inquiries using standardized scripts (Slack & Brandon-Jones, 2019). Another example is bank ATMs, which offer automated banking services for cash withdrawals, deposits, and transfers with limited personal interaction.

Next, I identified the five elements of business operations, which need to be considered in depth when developing a smooth and effective running of a company:

- **Layouts**: The layout of a facility, including equipment, workstations, and offices, is crucial for effective management. Proper design enhances efficiency, safety, and aesthetic appeal. It ensures smooth movement of materials, equipment, and personnel, minimising costs. Whether in a supermarket, restaurant, sports centre, or factory, even small layout changes can impact overall effectiveness and costs. Thoughtful planning of facility design is key to operational success (Slack & Brandon-Jones, 2019). Another example where layout is important can be hotels, where the focus is on the convenience and comfort of guests. This includes well-designed lobbies, guest rooms, conference areas, and recreational facilities. Thoughtful placement of amenities and clear wayfinding can significantly enhance guest satisfaction.

- **Supply chain management (SCM)**: SCM involves overseeing and optimising the entire process of producing and distributing a company's products. This includes transforming raw materials into final products and ensuring their efficient delivery to consumers. Effective SCM reduces waste, maximises customer value, and provides a competitive edge. It encompasses five key phases: planning, sourcing, production, distribution, and returns. While 'supply chain' refers to the linear flow of goods and information from suppliers to customers, 'supply network' includes all interconnected operations, and emphasises holistic management of resources and relationships (Slack & Brandon-Jones, 2019). Big fashion wear companies on High Street, supermarkets, and virtually all businesses have supply chains integral to their operations. These supply chains encompass the entire process, from the initial production of goods or services to their delivery to the end customer. Effective management of supply chains ensures that products are manufactured, distributed, and available to consumers efficiently and cost-effectively.

- **Lean Operations (Lean):** Lean operations aim to create value with minimal resources by reducing waste and inefficiencies. Key principles include meeting customer demand promptly, ensuring quality, and lowering costs. Concepts like 'just-in-time' (JIT) and the 'Toyota Production System' (TPS) are central to lean. By streamlining the flow of materials and information, lean reduces throughput time and minimises inventory. Examples include supermarkets restocking only when needed and construction companies scheduling material deliveries just in time. In education, lean allows for customised, rapid delivery of course materials (Slack & Brandon-Jones, 2019).

- **Total Quality Management (TQM):** TQM integrates quality efforts across an organization to produce economical goods and services while ensuring customer satisfaction. It emphasises meeting customer needs, involving all parts of the organisation, engaging every individual, analysing quality-related costs, and striving for accuracy. TQM also focuses on developing systems and procedures for continuous improvement (Slack & Brandon-Jones, 2019). An example of TQM implementation is in hospitals, where it aims to enhance patient care, minimize errors, and improve overall healthcare services. This process includes consistent staff training, ongoing monitoring of patient outcomes, and systematic enhancements of healthcare procedures.

- **Project Management:** Projects are defined activities with specific goals, clear timelines, and set resources. They range from organisational changes and R&D to large infrastructure projects. Projects are mission-focused, unique, and complex, leading to higher risks and uncertainties. Key stages in project management include understanding the environment, defining objectives, planning, technical execution, control, and learning from outcomes to improve future projects (Slack & Brandon-Jones, 2019). An example is software development projects, which involve creating or enhancing applications. The process includes gathering requirements, defining scope, planning, coding, testing, and deployment. Managing risks like changing requirements and technical challenges is crucial. Successful projects deliver a high-quality product that meets user needs.

My original curiosity on the topic grew into a keen interest, and I found this module particularly engaging. I was drawn to the concept and suddenly had a newfound respect for those bearing the title 'Operations Manager' once I had more understanding of the scale of their role within a business.

Our assignment for the module was to produce a 2500-word report that involved addressing two tasks related to a chosen company. The first task was relatively straightforward, involving the creation of an in-depth analysis. To complete the task, I needed to be thoroughly aware of the four essential topics:

- **Input-Transformation-Output Framework**: Understanding how inputs are transformed into outputs within operations.

- **The Four Vs**: These are volume, variety, variation, and viability—key factors that impact operations.

- **Operations Performance Objectives**: These include quality, speed, dependability, flexibility, and cost.

- **Order-Winners & Order-Qualifiers**: Factors that distinguish a company's offerings in the market.

For the second task, I focused on providing recommendations for my chosen industry. I decided to explore the operations management of the renowned fashion and retail company ZARA. Known for its diverse styles of designer clothes, ZARA caters not only to ladies' wear but also to men's and children's clothing (Slack & Brandon-Jones, 2019). Their unique blend of fashion-forward designs and accessibility has made them a global brand loved by many, myself included, which made researching more into the way the company works all the more interesting for me.

As I delved into my research, I realised that ZARA was more than just a fashion retailer - it had fascinating aspects related to supply chain management and manufacturing. ZARA's success is attributed to its unique business model, which includes four key processes: designing, production, sourcing, and retailing (Chu, 2005). Other critical factors for ZARA's success are speed, variety, affordable prices, flexibility, marketing, responsiveness, and brand image (Chu, 2005). As part of Inditex (Inditex.com)—the biggest fast fashion group in the world— ZARA follows vertical integration in its production steps. The initial input resources are raw materials like uncoloured fabrics, which can be dyed to match different trends (Zhelyazkov, 2023). The second set of inputs includes facilities and staff who handle designing, cutting, dyeing, ironing, packaging, labelling, quality control, distribution, and logistics using their own factories (Crofton & Dopico, 2007). Additionally, ZARA emphasises proximity by situating many of their end-product manufacturers close to their headquarters in Spain, Portugal, Turkey, and Morocco. This strategy helps them reduce energy consumption and minimise their carbon footprint. It also facilitates close collaboration with suppliers throughout the production process. By combining this proximity with short production runs, ZARA achieves exceptional flexibility and control, enabling them to produce a wide variety of sustainable and responsible fashion items (Inditex, 2024).

Having been previously unaware of the extensive background behind the clothing I purchase when shopping at ZARA, learning about how the garments travel along the supply train, evolving from raw materials to finished items along the way, was eye-opening. The intricacies of the numerous stages in the manufacturing process and the supply chain were a surprise at first, but understanding the importance of getting every detail right at each stage in the operation became clear.

As part of my coursework for 'Managing Business Operations,' I had an extra assignment that involved studying and revising for a practical test. The test came in the form of an oral exam, in which two questions on operations management topics would be selected by the examiners and students needed to verbally provide answers with relevant examples. We were given a total of nine minutes to find the answers to any two random questions from the 'Business Operations Management' topics, with four and a half minutes allocated for each question.

I diligently prepared for my practical test, and the questions that I was required to answer were on 'Types of Process' and 'Total Quality Management.' Using insights from the textbook *Operations Management* by Nigel Slack and Alistair Brandon- Jones (9th edition, 2019), I confidently answered both questions within the given time frame. The understanding I developed from this module spanned further than just what the role of an operations team is - it also shone a light onto just how complex the running of a large company or organisation is, and how many small components must be delicately balanced in order to pull off a project of any size. I found after a while that the way I looked at things had changed slightly, now that I had more of an understanding of the intricacies that go on behind the scenes of everything around us in all industries, and just how much work Operations Managers handle to keep businesses running smoothly. It certainly seemed like an area of work I could enjoy and had the skills to thrive in. The overall result of my written and practical assignments combined was a high 'B' grade, and my tutor commended my efforts and display of understanding.

Executing Business Strategy

Alongside the 'Managing Business Operations' module, I also studied 'Executing Business Strategy.' The title was new and intriguing, and my understanding of the module was mixed. A business strategy is a long-term plan that provides a broader perspective than some other definitions. For instance, a company might start by selling a single product and eventually expand to offer a wide range of services, both online and in physical stores. An organisation's long-term direction can include both planned strategies and those that emerge over time. It can also involve strategies aimed at differentiation and competition, as well as those that focus on collaboration and sometimes imitation (Whittington et al., 2021).

Additionally, I learned that a strategist's main task is to define and communicate a clear, motivating purpose for the organisation. In the private sector, this purpose often goes beyond just maximising profits, as long-term success and employee engagement usually require a mission that exceeds financial goals. The organisation's purpose should address two crucial questions: how does the organization make a difference, and who benefits from it?

In this module, I was introduced to the concepts of vision, mission, values, and Objectives, which were somewhat different from what I had learned in previous university modules. I believe these elements are vital for any company's success. When stakeholders align with a clear purpose, it can be very motivating. Organizations typically convey their purpose through:

- **Vision**: The long-term goals and aspirations that guide strategic decisions.

- **Mission**: The core activities, target audience, and main objectives of the organisation.

- **Values**: The fundamental principles that shape the organisation's culture and behaviour.

- **Objectives**: Organisations often set their goals using specific financial metrics, such as projected sales, profits, or share value over a defined period. They may also establish measurable market-based targets, like market share, customer satisfaction, and repeat business. Some objectives focus on competitive advantages; for example, a company might streamline operations to reduce costs and offer lower prices for cost leadership. Another objective could be market expansion by entering new geographic areas or segments to increase market share. Alternatively, a company might focus on differentiation by emphasising unique product features or superior quality to stand out in the market. Increasingly, organisations are adopting the 'triple bottom line' approach, setting goals that include economic outcomes as well as environmental and social responsibilities, reflecting a broader commitment to corporate social responsibility (Whittington et al., 2021).

Unlike the previous module, 'Executing Business Strategy' began by hitting us with a presentation, followed by a written assignment at a later date. I had spent the summer dreading hearing the word "presentation" pass my teacher's lips, but I knew it would only be a matter of time before it happened. Taking the initiative to seek help for my stammer over the summer had certainly made me feel more prepared, but I would have to wait a little longer before I could see if the speech therapy had paid off. Before we even got to start working on our presentations, a much more unforeseen adversary was flung our way: 'The Simulation Business Strategy Game.'

As the name suggests, the game is often used as a teaching or training tool, focusing on the multi-faceted nature of business strategy. For six weeks, our group participated in an online game as a fictional footwear company. I served as the CEO, while the other five team members took on roles such as Chief Financial Officer (CFO), Marketing Manager, HR Manager, and Operations Manager. Each week, we made decisions in various areas including management, purchasing, marketing (using the 4Ps: product, price, place, promotion), recruitment, and finance. Competing with other groups in our class, we reviewed the game's simulated results weekly and adjusted our strategies to address any weaknesses. Our team aimed to create a shoe company with a broad product range, focusing on offering luxury sports shoes for men, women, and children. We chose a growth strategy centred on developing new products for existing markets. This approach allowed us to refine our competitive strategy for product leadership, ensuring we offered the highest quality shoes in the market.

From the outset, I grappled with understanding the processes of 'The Simulation Business Strategy Game.' The very word 'online' instantly triggered a lurch in my stomach. I had been working consistently on my computing skills since the start of my studies but was finding my progress quite slow. Despite years of online classes, video calls, written reports, and modules encompassing technology and computers in a variety of ways, this had been the area that had taken the most adapting to.

Somehow, the keys and the clicks were not forming muscle memory reactions or becoming instinctive. The progress was there, but nowhere near as fast as I would have liked. My difficulties emphasised the need to keep up to date with progress in order to stay in tune with the evolving world. Technology is constantly making advancements, and though it is often easier to ignore this or brush it off as something that doesn't apply to us. The reality is that to stay ahead, you have to stay in touch with progress. The world of computers and technology plays a huge part in life, particularly in business, and if you don't keep evolving with it, you will get left behind. I regretted the fact that I had not foreseen that I might need computer literacy in the future, and as a result, aspects of my life were much more difficult. Trying to learn decades of technological advancement in one go it might hard than keeping in touch with progress as it comes. This gaping blind spot in my skillset had once again come back to bite me, but as easy as it is to regret, it is more important to focus on allowing ourselves to learn as we go. So, I vowed to keep up my efforts to learn how to use technology, and from there, keep in touch with its evolution.

To add to the pressure, I was then appointed as the Chief Executive Officer in the simulation game, a role which also came with the task of starting the group presentation. It wasn't until we started delving into the online game that it then hit me how heavily it also incorporated my old nemesis: mathematics. I almost choked, feeling panic clawing at my throat. Those three elements—computers, public speaking, and mathematics—were my trifecta of failure. But the panic did not last long. I refused to allow it to. I knew that this was a pivotal moment for me, and that I had to keep my head screwed on and use everything the previous three years had taught me about the topics and about myself if I intended to succeed. I felt utterly overfaced, as though this could very well end in disaster, but I was also resolute to give it my best try.

There is not a person on the planet who is completely without weakness. In fact, every single one of us has dozens of weaknesses. I had come to accept my weaknesses, embracing asking for help and understanding ways to counter them, however, having my three biggest foes combined was not what I was expecting to see. Nevertheless, I forced myself to find the silver lining. Surely, if I could conquer a project that was so heavily stacked against me, then in the future, I would have no need to fear any of these topics by themselves.

My team members steamed ahead of me, able to grasp the concepts with what seemed like relative ease. It appeared clear from where I was standing that they had much more advanced knowledge of math and technology, and though I tried not to, I admittedly felt inferior. They adeptly navigated the online learning resource, swiftly locating answers and financial figures. Participating in decision-making within the group simulation at the same time as feeling as though I understood significantly less than everyone else made me feel like a fraud. Finding accurate information from within the game, analysing financial sheets, and understanding profit and loss felt like guesswork and interpreting the data to determine the company's profit and loss was extremely difficult for me. I began to sense that my teammates were noticing my shortcomings. Struggling to find market share data, I at one point selected incorrect information. Fortunately, one of my peers guided me in locating the necessary financial details to create a bar chart for the market share, but similar situations still arose. The task of visualising financial results through charts and graphs felt daunting, especially since the other students in my group made it look so easy and were repeatedly coming to my aid, but I decided to take the pressure as a driving force, rather than an excuse to fail.

In the previous three years of studying, math-related modules had always been my least favourite. Struggling through 'Data Skills,' 'Business Finance,' and 'Economics for Business' had me feeling well out of my depth. However, 'Executing Business Strategy' was topping them all. As this project required working as part of a group, I realised that although my teammates were more advanced than me in all areas, they were also busy with their own roles, and I didn't feel that it was fair to expect them to carry me through, too. The feeling of inferiority got to me—how could I play the part of the CEO in the game when I felt like I had less to contribute to a team? It was time to use my initiative and take positive action.

I sought help from an online Math tutor who was skilled in ICT packages, business, and especially Excel. By now, I had a clear understanding of the value of seeking help in the right places, and the shame I had once had when it came to asking for assistance was significantly diminished. With the tutor's steady guidance, I learned to create charts and graphs step by step. These visual tools were directly related to financial data, such as gross revenue, sales growth, inventory turnover, working capital turnover, overall leverage ratio, and stock out. Additionally, she explained the meaning of each financial metric to me, ensuring that I would be able to understand every graph, chart or collection of data that was put before me.

Beyond mastering the technical aspects, I understood the importance of each graph within a business. I could assess the business's performance and identify weaknesses in various areas. Thanks to my wonderful tutor and her passionate support, the concepts, calculations, and translation of information into Excel charts no longer felt like a nightmare to me. My experiences when it came to reaching out for extra guidance had taught me that we are not inferior to experts, or those who seem ahead - they have simply mastered what we have not yet had a chance to experience. With patience and perseverance, we can take even the challenges that feel huge, or make us feel small, and turn them into experience and understanding. We gain nothing from feeling inferior but have everything to gain from taking that feeling and turning it into personal improvement.

The simulation business our group created was a footwear company named Diamond. Part of my role as CEO in the simulation came with producing various graphs and charts to show the company's growth and development, and with thanks to my online private tutor, I was not only able to generate effective and accurate graphs, but I was also able to fully understand them. I no longer needed to rely on my peers to carry me through these aspects of my role in the group and had become a clear contributor to our efforts.

I have included some examples of the charts and graphs I prepared for the simulation. These visual tools offer valuable insights into the business's health and performance:

Figure 5: Executing Business Strategy, Market Share, November 2023

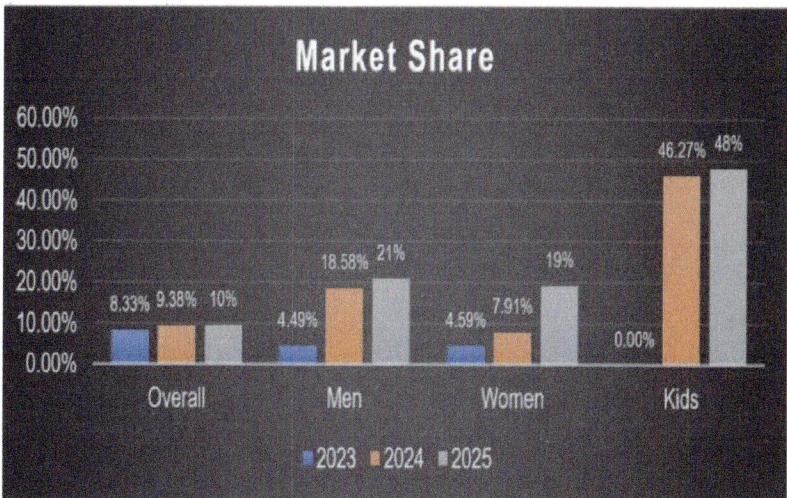

Source: Created and presented by Yusra Mariyam

Figure 6: Executing Business Strategy Presentation, Sales in Pounds, November 2023

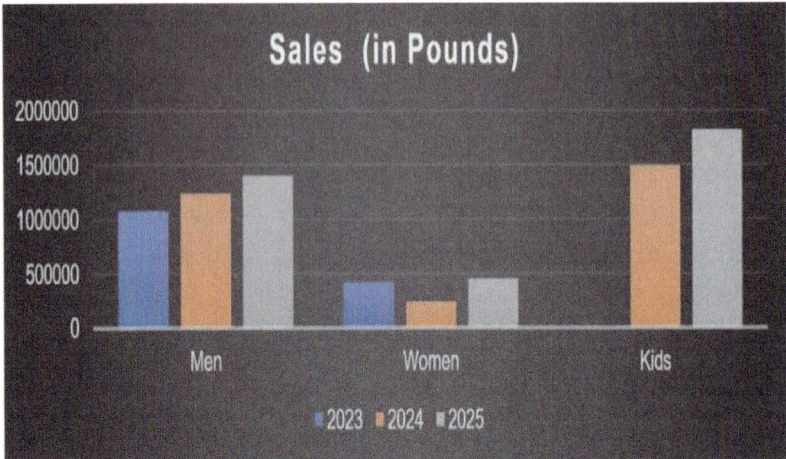

Source: Created and presented by Yusra Mariyam

Figure 7: Executing Business Strategy Presentation, Overall Working Capital Turnover Ratio, November 2023

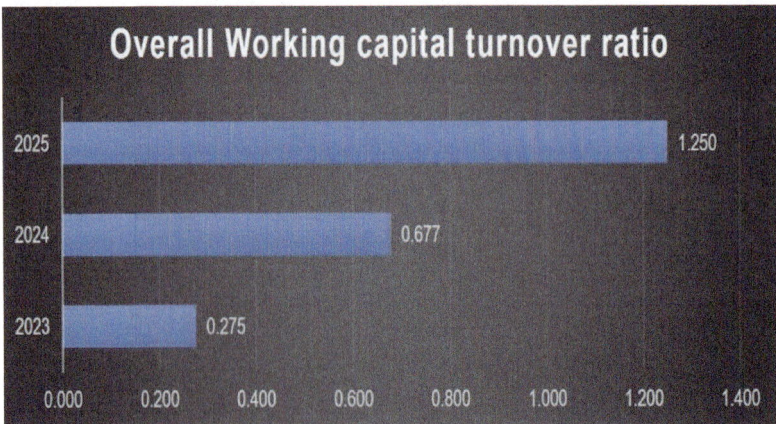

Source: Created and presented by Yusra Mariyam

Figure 8: Executing Business Strategy Presentation, Stock Out in units, November 2023

Source: Created and presented by Yusra Mariyam

Figure 9: Executing Business Strategy Presentation, Stock Out in units, November 2023

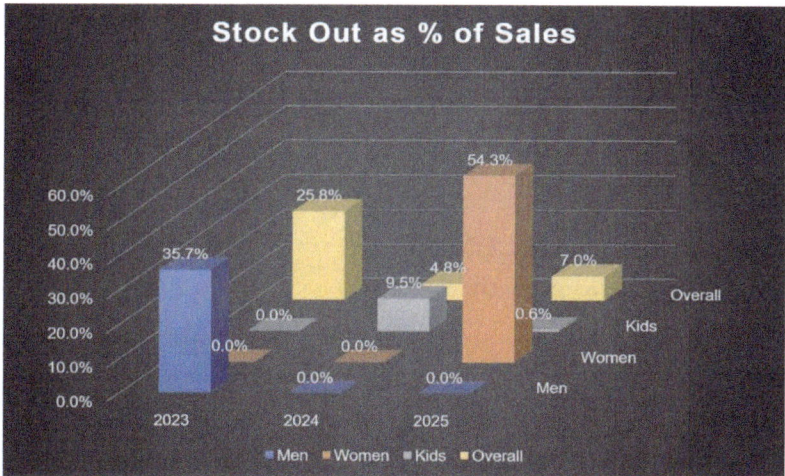

Source: Created and presented by Yusra Mariyam

In November 2023, I was well-prepared for my presentation for the 'Executing Business Strategy' module, based around Diamond Footwear—the company my team had created using the business simulator. In my role, I had to cover specific key points that would convey valuable information about Diamond Footwear, and here's what I included in my presentation:

Company Snapshot and Marketplace Position:

- Outlining where my company stands in the market.
- Providing a snapshot of its current position.

Company Details:

- Vision and Mission: Sharing my company's overarching goals and purpose.
- Core Values: Highlighting the principles that guide my company's actions.
- Performance Objectives: Setting clear targets for my company's success.

Financial Performance:

- Discussing financial metrics, including revenue, loss, profit, and growth.
- Analysing my company's financial health.

Industry Trends and Change Drivers:

- Identifying the four major factors influencing the footwear industry, using economic, social, technological, and legal factors.

- Explaining how these trends impact the business.

Strategic Decisions:

- Outlining my company's strategic choices.

- Discussing my business's generic competitive strategies, market growth strategy, and corporate strategy.

Overall, the final presentation provided a comprehensive view of the company's performance, strategy, and competitive edge. The presentation was a team effort, performed in front of our tutor in a face-to-face assessment. As the CEO, I had to speak first. I presented the 'Diamond' footwear company's position in a snapshot of the marketplace, and it was imperative that I covered each point in detail, ensuring that I displayed my understanding and my contribution to the team. I took a deep breath, drawing on what I had learned during my speech therapy session, and began. As I spoke, I surprised myself by how my words flowed and how composed I seemed, despite feeling like my heart might burst from my chest at any moment.

Time seemed to speed up and slow down at the same time, and before I knew it, my role in the presentation was over. Following my part of the presentation, the HR Manager presented the competitive position of the company. The Marketing Manager then presented the strengths and weaknesses of the company, the CFO presented the strategic opportunities to unlock growth, and lastly, the Operations Manager presented the sustainability strategy to drive positive change for the company. Each role was equally important, clearly representing the need for a well- functioning cooperative team in order to allow a business strategy to run smoothly.

I was awarded a 'B' grade for my role in the presentation, of which I was exceptionally proud. The project had thrown all of my major limitations at me in one go, but I realised, in hindsight, that it was exactly what I needed at the time. This presentation had been the biggest task so far in my degree, and though I was glad it was over, I was excited by the personal Goliath I had just slain. Three years prior, when I had first started my degree, the very thought of a project like this would have made me crumble and run for cover. I suddenly appreciated how the process of studying had truly honed my resilience. Though the challenge itself had been daunting, the true lesson lay in the value of not giving up. Within each of us, there is something we feel is beyond our reach. Something too high to climb, too big to battle or even too shameful to seek assistance for, but this is simply not the case. Seeing my three biggest weaknesses sitting before me turned out to be a defining moment in my studies, and a shift in my mindset. Therefore, when your personal mountain blocks your path, don't stop where you are; look for other paths, climb over the peak or even dig a tunnel through, but don't stand still. Every problem has a solution, it just takes perseverance to find it sometimes.

After completing the 'Executing Business Strategy' presentation, I then faced a 3000-word assignment. The assignment involved discussing three points based on the online business simulation game:

- I needed to evaluate the Strategic Management, Business Model, and Performance. In this section, I outlined Diamond Footwear's vision, mission, core values, and performance objectives. I also detailed the four major decisions made during the six-week simulation and created a balanced scorecard. This scorecard presented my company's strategic objectives across financial, customer, internal process, and learning areas.

- I needed to analyse the Business Environments: In this section, I conducted a SWOT analysis for our Diamond Footwear, assessing its strengths, weaknesses, opportunities, and threats. Additionally, I applied Porter's 'Five Forces Framework' to evaluate the industry, identifying key competitive forces such as the threat of new entrants, the bargaining power of buyers and suppliers, the threat of substitutes, and the intensity of competitive rivalry (Whittington et al., 2021). The focus was on using these internal and external business environment analysis frameworks for Diamond Footwear.

- I needed to assess strategic priorities for innovation. I emphasised the importance of innovation, suggesting that the Internet of Things (IoT) could improve inventory management by enabling remote control and tracking through automated systems. This technology allows for the monitoring and location of all assets, from raw materials to large warehouse equipment (Vas, 2020). Additionally, I pointed out that Artificial Intelligence (AI) could replace employees with virtual assistants, such as online chatbots, to provide 24/7 customer support, thereby reducing costs by eliminating the need for human presence (Pantano & Pizzi, 2020). These chatbots can mimic human conversations, offering logical and effective online customer experiences. As part of this, I recommended that our Diamond Footwear expands its sneaker business in the USA as part of its growth strategy, particularly as the company increases sales and achieves long-term profitability.

Thankfully, this part of the module felt easy following the mammoth task my team had just completed. Accompanied by the textbook *Fundamentals of Strategy, fifth edition,* authored by Richard Whittington, Patrick Regnér, Duncan Angwin, Gerry Johnson, and Kevan Scholes, 2021, I was able to draw information from both the simulation game and my presentation, which assisted me in completing all tasks required for this module.

My overall performance in the module, combining both the assignment and presentation, saw me land just four marks away from an 'A' grade. Comparing the two modules of my first semester—'Managing Business Operations' and 'Executing Business Strategy'—I felt much more confident in the former than in the latter. Achieving a firm 'B' grade in both, despite how negatively I felt about 'Executing Business Strategy,' gave me something to reflect upon. This experience taught me the importance of not being overconfident, even when tasks seem easier, and striving for excellence regardless of perceived difficulty. My fear of failure when faced with my 'Business Strategy' presentation resulted in me reaching out for extra help, applying intense focus to learning and tackling some of my biggest weaknesses, and the result was success. In contrast, feeling so comfortable in the realm of the 'Managing Business Operations' assignment resulted in less drive behind my efforts, and though I still succeeded, my final score was a few points less than that of the module I struggled with. Putting in equal effort and dedication, even when we feel we are not faced with a challenge, will reap even greater rewards.

Although the challenges in 'Executing Business Strategy' were tough, the group presentation taught me another valuable lesson: to find my own support in the right places rather than relying on others. Though my team had more advanced skills than I did in certain elements, it was not their responsibility to teach me, and it would not be fair of me to expect them to. I could see how this echoed navigating life itself, emphasising the importance of analysing both positive and negative situations, considering internal and external factors, identifying gaps or opportunities, and working on those areas for improvement. Knowing when to reach out for help and the appropriate way to get it is important. Though assistance and guidance from those around us is something of great value, fairness comes from remembering that others also have their own roles, problems, and things to do. Expecting them to carry you, even if they seem as though they are ahead or would find it easy, is not always conducive to personal growth. Abba often told me, "Don't depend on others. You must handle your own responsibilities. Never just expect someone else to do it for you." He emphasised that in order to be a contributory member of a group, you must grow yourself independently, too. This applies to all facets of life - it could be a team at work, it could be with your family, or in your community. Self-reliant development is just as important as working together.

After a demanding three months, my first semester concluded in mid-December 2023, and classes paused for a few weeks. I was well used to the format of university life by now. However, this semester break was different. I was also not oblivious to the fact that this would be my final winter break and that the end of my course was now very much within sight.

Semester 2

For four years, January had consistently marked the start of the familiar pattern— winter break was coming to an end, and I was once again gearing up for resuming studies and facing the two final modules left ahead of me. Each year, the start of the second semester had brought the swirl of enthusiasm and anticipation that I had now come to quite enjoy, but this year there was a very different blend of emotions bubbling below the surface. Suddenly, I found that deeper feelings had jumped into the mix: fear, hope, anger, sadness—my focus was no longer only on the semester ahead, but on the uncertain road that lay beyond. I had put so much time and effort into this degree, but what would come next? What doors would swing open and welcome me inside? I am sure all students experience some version of this. The relief at the prospect of ending ongoing presentations and assignments, the mind racing with questions or the fear of falling at the final hurdle. Nevertheless, this is what I had been working toward, so I had to regain control and get my head back in the game.

On a crisp Saturday in January 2024, I returned to university for the start of my second semester of the academic year. In fact, the eighth semester of my education, which seemed like a staggering achievement. As I stepped into the classroom, I observed my classmates—smartly dressed, faces beaming with smiles. Some exchanged hugs, others greeted with handshakes, and lengthy conversations filled the air as they caught up after the month-long break. Though on the surface we all looked calm, I couldn't help but wonder who else had a head full of contradicting emotions and a fizzing of fear.

In the heart of the room stood a new gentleman, his glasses perched on his nose, and lines of experience etched into his face. He wore a broad, welcoming smile that instantly put everyone at ease. His gaze, calm and discerning, swept across the faces entering and settling down. I identified him as the module's new teacher, and once the students were in their seats and the greetings subsided, he took the lead. He introduced himself and provided essential details about the new module: 'Critical Perspectives on Cross-Border Business.' Following that, he grouped everyone and assigned one member from each group to introduce their fellow classmates—sharing names, occupations, and backgrounds. We learned that this teacher would be guiding us in both morning and afternoon classes, offering some consistency, which I quietly found a little comforting. I realised that this man was my final guide along this stretch of my journey and into my hard-earned future.

Critical Perspectives on Cross-Border Business

As the Saturday classes unfolded each week, the teacher provided increasing details about the module, which in return provided increasing confusion for me. The concept of

'Managing Cross-Border Business' was unsurprisingly complex, and the structure of the assignment itself was an intricate puzzle. As the name suggested, this module explored international business, specifically focusing on IKEA—the world-famous Swedish seller of flat-packed furniture. The assignment focused initially on IKEA's presence in Japan and the broader Asian region.

Now, let's zero in on the actual assignment task: we were to identify, outline, and critically evaluate IKEA's international expansion. My focus lay in understanding how IKEA operates as an innovative, environmentally sustainable business in Japan and the Asian region, and how the company was able to expand to this area successfully. I also needed to conduct extensive research and uncover IKEA's management practices. This would involve discussing various aspects such as design, production, foreign direct investment, joint ventures, management information systems, logistics, marketing, branding, and sales. It was hard to know where to start—there was so much information to seek. I had no idea which section to focus on first, where to find the information or how to piece it all together correctly.

Our teacher was ready to help, having already laid out a comprehensive structure for us to use as guidance. This roadmap provided clear direction on where to begin, what information to gather, and how to proceed. Even the specific topics and titles to explore were included. I was grateful for such a clear starting point, something that I had struggled with in some of the previous assignments. Indeed, armed with this structured approach, I felt a sense of contentment and self-certainty. It was almost as though the teacher had echoed IKEA's flat-pack furniture process, giving us comprehensive instructions, all the parts to the puzzle, and advice on how to build it all together, slotting each piece into the right place using the right tools, until a perfectly constructed report came to fruition. While I anticipated a long and challenging journey, my determination would guide me through.

I began my 'Cross-Border' assignment by following the guidelines and structure provided by my teacher. My starting point focused on the background of IKEA, which was founded by a seventeen-year-old named Ingvar Kamprad in 1943 as a mail-order company. The first physical store opened in Sweden in 1958 (Hill,2021). My assignment delved into various aspects of IKEA, of course including a focus on its presence in Asia, and particularly in Japan. I meticulously analysed the company using several models.

Although I had encountered some of these models before, this module required a deeper dive to fully understand the factors related to each model and how to apply them to thoroughly examine IKEA. To answer the assignment questions and gather the expanses of relevant information required, I realised that a comprehensive understanding of the models and their application was crucial. Therefore, I delved into these factors more extensively than I had done previously, holding a magnifying glass to the intricacies of the process. I was nearing the end of my university journey, and I was struck by the realisation of how much I had learned. Had I been faced with this challenge just a few years ago, I would have had no clue where to begin. However, though I was not completely confident in my abilities, I was ready to put my knowledge to the test.

Here is a list of the models I researched, based on my newfound understanding:

- **Porter's Five Forces**: I analysed the industry's competitive dynamics, considering elements like supplier power, buyer power, competitive rivalry, the threat of substitutes, and the threat of new entrants (Whittington et al., 2021).

- **Porter's Diamond Model Theory**: I explored the determinants of national competitive advantage, including elements like factor conditions, demand conditions, related and supporting industries, and firm strategy, structure, and rivalry (Review, 2024).

- **PESTLE Analysis**: I considered the political, economic, social, technological, legal, and environmental factors affecting IKEA's operations in Japan and Asia (Shaw, 2024).

- **Hofstede Cultural Factors**: I examined how IKEA adapted to cultural differences between Sweden and Japan. Understanding cultural dimensions can be crucial for successful international business (The Culture Factor Group, 2024).

Additionally, I investigated IKEA's competitive advantage strategy to uncover the reasons behind the company's success. An interesting fact emerged during my research: IKEA initially entered the Japanese market in 1974 through a joint venture, but this attempt was unsuccessful, leading to its withdrawal from Japan (Leroux et al., 2007). However, IKEA didn't give up on Japan. In 2006, they made a second entry, learning from their previous mistakes. This time, they conducted thorough research, visited Japanese consumer homes and offices, and studied Japanese culture and lifestyle. The structured approach allowed IKEA to succeed in Japan by understanding and meeting Japanese consumer needs and expectations (Retail Revival in Japan, 2024). Without prior research or an understanding of the market, IKEA had been unable to adjust its conduct according to the needs of the customer during their first attempt at expansion. I also learned about Foreign Direct Investment in international countries; a way of ensuring thorough research, customer attraction, and adherence to local regulations would significantly contribute to success.

I diligently continued my explorations of IKEA by exploring additional research models and conducting further analyses. Some of the models I utilised included:

- **Uppsala Model and Psychic Distance**: These frameworks help me to understand how firms internationalise and the role of cultural and geographical factors in their decision-making process (Hill, 2021).

- **Greenfield Investment**: This model supported me to investigate the advantages and disadvantages of establishing new operations (such as factories or offices) in foreign countries from scratch (Thakur, 2023).

- **Kearney's Foreign Direct Investment (FDI) Confidence Index**: This index assesses the appeal of different countries for investment. By applying this model, I determined the attractiveness of different countries for my research, which helped me complete my assignment on foreign direct investment (FDI) (Peterson & Toland, 2023).

- **Grand Strategy Matrix**: This tool assisted me in evaluating strategic options by considering market growth and competitive position (GetLucidity.com).

- **Environmental, Social, and Governance (ESG)**: This required me to consider IKEA's sustainability practices and ethical responsibilities (What is ESG? A guide for businesses, 2023).

- **Sustainable Development Goals (SDGs)**: These global goals aim to address social, economic, and environmental challenges, and I explored how IKEA aligns with them (Sustainable Development Goals, 2024).

- **Triple Bottom Line (TBL)**: This involved an analysis into IKEA's performance in terms of economic, social, and environmental impact (Triple Bottom Line, 2023).

Supported by my tutor's meticulous instructions and the textbook *International Business: Competing in the Global Marketplace 13th edition*, authored by Charles W.

L. Hill in 2021, I combined theoretical frameworks with practical insights to create a comprehensive analysis of IKEA's global operations. My assignment also included findings related to international trade agreements. Here are the key agreements I examined and my explanation of each:

- **General Agreement on Tariffs and Trade (GATT):** GATT was an international treaty designed to lower trade barriers, such as tariffs, and foster global economic cooperation. It laid the groundwork for the establishment of the World Trade Organization (WTO).

- **World Trade Organization (WTO):** The WTO is an international body that regulates trade rules and negotiations. It offers a framework for resolving trade disputes and promotes free and fair trade among its member nations.

- **Free Trade Agreements (FTAs):** I examined specific FTAs relevant to IKEA's operations. These agreements ease trade by lowering or removing tariffs and other barriers between member countries. By considering these agreements, I gained insights into the regulatory landscape that impacts IKEA's global business activities.

Without realising how much I was enjoying it, I delved head-first into the research project, absorbing everything I could along the way. My research journey seemed endless, with countless models and secondary analyses. The word count ballooned to over 15,000 words, far exceeding the initial 3,000-word briefing. I had gained so much understanding, examined so many areas, and explored every angle our teacher had directed us toward, and as a result, rather than struggling to put together a 3,000-word essay, I was struggling to whittle the information down enough to fit it all in. My classmates dropped me a valuable tip: information presented in tables wouldn't be counted toward the word limit. I strategically summarised much of my analysis, findings, and conclusions within those tables, removing them from the body of the piece. This allowed me to meet the assignment requirements while showcasing my thorough understanding of the subject matter.

I had surprised myself with my success in this assignment, pulling out the stops and producing my best work yet, whilst enjoying every minute of it. Seeing my word count hit 15,000 and knowing that I understood every sentence in detail left me feeling empowered. It is incredible how our inner strengths can surprise us when we push ourselves beyond our comfort zones. New or forgotten talents or interests can pop up out of the blue, enriching our journey of self-discovery. For example, my writing skills, developed during my school years, had gained new significance as I pursued my International Business Management degree. I suddenly recovered a passion that I had left behind so long ago and was now relishing written assignments. Life often presents opportunities at just the right moment, helping us uncover hidden aptitudes and strengths—much like I did during this assignment. I recognised that my drive for excellence and my relentless efforts were uncovering so much more for me than just business knowledge, and this only made me increasingly ready to tackle anything that was to come my way.

The next part of our 'Cross-Border' module was a role-playing assignment—far from what I was expecting. At first, the value of the task wasn't clear. After all, this course was for a degree in international business management, not performing arts! With a little more explanation, however, the relevance of the task became clearer.

The exercise involved six participants per group, each with an assigned role to play. I was to portray a local supplier for the fictional Japanese EV manufacturer 'PANOSHIBA,' based in Sunderland. In the scenario, PANOSHIBA was considering relocating from the UK to other European countries due to various challenges that had emerged post-Brexit in December 2020. My fellow participants and I were tasked with convincing the PANOSHIBA EV Plant to stay in the UK by presenting compelling arguments that highlighted the profitability, strategic benefits, and opportunities of remaining. Each of these points would need to be backed up with research, evidence, and data in order to build a sturdy argument. To bolster my case, I conducted extensive research using secondary sources and employed a range of strategic business tools, including:

- **S.W.O.T Analysis** to identify the company's strengths, weaknesses, opportunities, and threats.

- **Hofstede's Cultural Dimensions** to compare cultural differences between the UK and Japan.

- **Thomas-Kilmann Conflict Model** to understand conflict resolution approaches (Mishra et al., 2021).

- **Mendelow's Matrix** for stakeholder analysis in order to understand interests and roles of different stakeholders (Barrington, 2024).

- **Porter's Diamond Model** to evaluate competitive advantages (Model & Lopez, 2023).

- **BATNA** to determine the best alternatives outside of a negotiated agreement (Batna, 2023).

In my assigned role as a domestic supplier, I provided numerous persuasive points to encourage PANOSHIBA to stay in the UK, backing my points with clear and comprehensive research. My preferred outcome, as per BATNA, was for the company to remain in the UK to ensure market continuity, leverage the skilled workforce for rapid production scaling, and align with the government's green economy initiatives. However, my BATNA also prepared me for the worst-case scenario: if PANOSHIBA decided to leave, I was ready to continue supplying their operations in mainland Europe, albeit with new challenges and strategies, such as partnering with new local suppliers, renegotiating contracts, and exploring shipping options.

As it turned out, I found that role-playing as a domestic supplier was immensely helpful, opening my eyes to a new area of the supply chain. It positively impacted my existing professional role in sales, enhancing my communication, rapport-building, influence, and negotiation skills. Before the task, I had a limited understanding of supply chain management, but through the role-play, and extensive research, I gained a comprehensive understanding, and fresh insights, into the role of a supplier, putting myself in their shoes and learning the intricacies of their part in the process. Carrying this experience into my full-time job had an instant positive impact on my work performance. I saw the advantages of understanding the ins and outs of the roles of colleagues and peers and how this knowledge could benefit the entire team or chain, not just myself.

Upon completing the 'Cross-Border' module, I found that it had been an exceptionally enjoyable and engaging experience. It stood out as my favourite among all the modules I had undertaken throughout my degree programme. The assignments had been challenging and with a high workload, and the role-play was new territory for me, but the module had also forced me to persevere, despite being faced with unique challenges and large amounts of time-consuming research. It had required me to tap into my ability to persevere, and I was rewarded with a deeper comprehension of International Business Management and higher performance in my existing job.

While I had a keen interest in 'Global Debates' during my foundation year, and 'Legal Aspect of Business' in my second year, the 'Cross-Border Business' module emerged as the most enlightening and fulfilling one I had encountered. My natural curiosity found that researching had been particularly engaging, and my multicultural background meant that I had some existing understanding of international dynamics and the importance of understanding other cultures, especially when it comes to integration. This module sang to my existing skills and interests more than I had expected it to, and I believe that the teacher played a crucial role in my success. By providing a structured outline of topics to cover in each section of the assignment and offering a clear starting point, he had given us a better chance to flourish and ensure a true understanding of what was required of us. I couldn't help but appreciate the contrast between the teachers of my final year in high school and my teacher during my final year at university.

Undergraduate Major Project (Leadership in Practice)

My journey through the 'Cross-Border' assignment had been both demanding and rewarding. Now, as I entered the final module of my second semester—the 'Undergraduate Major Project (Leadership in Practice)'—I encountered a familiar face. The same teacher who guided us through 'Legal Aspects of Business' during the second year of the degree course was to be leading this module. It was a big relief, knowing that I wouldn't have to adjust to a new teacher's style, and could focus on the task at hand. The 'Legal Aspects of Business' module had been enjoyable, not just because of my keen interest in law, but because this tutor was helpful, entertaining, and effective when conveying knowledge. I was comforted by the knowledge that we were in good hands. However, this new module would require me to harness every ounce of resilience and tenacity I could muster in order to conquer the final hurdle that stood between me and my degree: the viva.

The viva is essentially a presentation, but without any slides. It is an oral examination where the teacher gives the student a topic to write about and present. This allows the examiners to assess the understanding and depth of knowledge on a specific subject or research project. I had to prepare my presentation on the leadership theories of a company of my choice, opting to focus on Rolls-Royce. I had to use an array of facts and data in my piece, but all information needed to be cited, proving my extensive research and understanding. Ideally, all of this needed to be learned from memory where possible, to display that we had clearly learned this information and could recall it quickly. Different to the presentations I had previously been part of during my final year, the viva would be quite lengthy, and I would be doing it alone. The results would be a major factor in my final grade, so there would be no room for error.

I soon discovered that preparing for the viva would not be as straightforward as the initial briefing suggested. As I delved deeper into the details of the task, I realised that this journey would require adaptability and initiative, and that I would have to draw on every skill I had developed during my course if I was to succeed.

The 'Undergraduate Major Project (Leadership in Practice)' module explored various leadership theories that describe the diverse leadership and management styles inherent in professionals' and individuals' personalities. It encompasses a variety of theories that I set out to explore, which are included below:

- **'The Great Man Theories,'** which assert that leadership abilities are inherent, suggesting that certain individuals are naturally equipped with traits that make them effective leaders.

- **'Trait Theories,'** which emphasise the particular personality traits and characteristics that contribute to effective leadership.

- **'Behaviour Theories,'** which examine the actions and behaviours of leaders rather than their traits or circumstances.

- **'Situational Theories,'** which propose that effective leadership is contingent upon the situation at hand.

- **'Relational Theories,'** which emphasise the importance of the relationships between leaders and their followers.

- **'New Leadership Approaches,'** which introduce contemporary concepts and practices in leadership.

- **'Emerging Leadership Approaches,'** which explore the evolving trends and future directions of leadership theory.

These valuable insights were new to me and were derived from my module teacher's teachings, further supported by key textbooks: *Introduction to Leadership, Concepts and Practice* (5th Edition) by Peter G. Northouse (2021), *The Theory and Practice of Change Management* (6th Edition) by John Hayes (2022), and *Leadership for Organizations* by David A. Waldman and Charles O'Reilly (2020)

I devoted myself to preparing my viva presentation for the module, concentrating on leadership theories and styles as exemplified by Rolls-Royce. My enthusiasm for this specific company had been consistent, having previously presented on Rolls- Royce in my first-year 'Business Environment' module, and as such, I was already quite familiar with the company and its dealings. For my viva, I honed in on various leadership approaches and styles demonstrated within the company, such as:

- **Transformational Leadership**: Focusing on inspiring change and innovation.

- **Strategic Leadership**: Emphasising long-term vision and company direction.

- **Operational Leadership**: Dealing with day-to-day management and operations.

- **Pragmatic Leadership**: Being practical and results-oriented.

- **Inclusive Leadership**: Ensuring diversity and participation.

- **Servant Leadership**: Prioritising the needs of employees and customers.

- **Ethical Leadership**: Upholding moral standards and integrity.

Additionally, I incorporated studies on concepts such as negotiation principles, emotional intelligence, and communication methods to provide a comprehensive view of leadership within the context of Rolls-Royce and what makes it so successful. Although through experience I had a natural understanding of leadership, as we are all granted by social norms, discovering its various definitions and traits was both intriguing and beneficial. It helped me appreciate that people in different environments—whether at work, in educational institutions, or at home—exhibit a wide range of leadership skills.

As part of my exploration, I also examined numerous leadership skills employed by various companies. This included a look at transformative leadership theories that adapt to new skills like technological solutions, climate change responses, and employee empowerment. This is supported by Sliwka et al. (2023), who state that transformational leadership inspires staff to enhance their tasks, fosters innovation, develops a shared vision, and builds trust and collaboration.

During my viva, I also discussed three other leadership skills: Strategic Leadership, which fosters strong workplace cultures and behaviours (Waldman & O'Reilly, 2020), Operational Leadership, which is characterized by strong character and mental agility rather than being innate traits (Vego, 2015), and Pragmatic Leadership, which requires extensive knowledge of economic issues, critical thinking, and expertise to navigate crises and achieve goals based on threats and opportunities (Anderson & Sun, 2015).

Throughout my four-year degree, I encountered various presentations and struggled with almost all of them. My stammer repeatedly tripped me up and flustered me, leaving me to rely on my notes and struggling through it. However, I had spent the summer equipping myself with techniques and know-how that would banish my stammer. I knew that the viva presentation was vital for succeeding in my degree, so it would be time to truly put my practice to use. The presentation included very specific requirements: I needed to cite references for each statement I made about the leadership styles associated with Rolls-Royce. Backing up everything I said with factual evidence was imperative but also added a lot of pressure. I would have to put in hours of revision to ensure that I gave myself the best chance of recalling information and thus reduce the need to check my notes—a previous shortcoming of mine.

My presentation was slightly over 900 words and had to be delivered in seven minutes. Remembering every detail was strikingly difficult, so I brought notes to assist me, although I made a concerted effort to engage with my body language and maintain eye contact with the teacher to avoid appearing as though I was merely reading from the script. I recalled my speech therapist's advice and practised the presentation several times, filming myself and rewatching it to see where I was struggling the most. I did my best to mirror the speaking style of Barack Obama, as I had been taught, echoing his delivery and confidence. In the past, relying on notes during presentations had had a detrimental impact on my grades, but given that this presentation was much longer than my previous ones and required a lot more facts to be worked into it, I still felt more comfortable knowing that I had them at hand if I got stuck.

I was hopeful for a positive outcome, trusting that my efforts would be reflected in my grade, but I would have to wait until the end of the semester to receive feedback on my viva. In the end, I felt pretty good about my performance. I had provided many theories on leadership, spoken clearly and loudly, used expressions and gestures when I was speaking, and avoided tripping up over my words. On the downside, I had also had to check my notes a small handful of times, which I knew I would lose points for, but had been unavoidable in the moment. I managed to perform my 900-word presentation within the seven-minute timeframe, whilst needing to not only recall the piece itself, but also remember to pay extra attention to every part of my body in order to stave off my stammer.

To my surprise, I found the viva experience to be highly enjoyable. It had been the perfect opportunity to test-drive my public speaking skills in a solo presentation, though the aspect of referencing my sources during the presentation added an extra layer of difficulty to the assignment. I welcomed the chance to demonstrate my adaptability and rise to the new challenge. Upon completing the viva assignment, I believed I had finished all my tasks for the semester. However, I was soon informed that one more remained: a leadership assignment.

This task felt much different from the various other assignments that we had been given over the years. It required introspection, focusing on my personal leadership qualities and how they relate to my job and industry. At first, I thought it would be straightforward. After all, who knows me better than I do? But once I sat down to begin, I realised this was not the case. Describing others or evaluating a company is one thing, but self-assessing my own leadership strengths and weaknesses presented a much more significant challenge.

My goal was to pinpoint and express the leadership skills I'd applied in my professional journey so far, looking at my full-time job in particular. I had to select two out of four key experiences to discuss in my professional role for this assignment. I opted to focus on resilience and communication, both of which were essential skills I regularly employed in my sales position. These skills are not just part of my job - they are crucial for my success and effectiveness in my field, and over time have become second nature to me in my professional setting.

I began my final leadership assignment by reflecting on my work experience, starting in September 2017. I explored how I practised resilience and communication at work, drawing on 'Mason's Resilience Model' to illustrate my approach to overcoming challenges, gaining support, nurturing positivity, staying healthy, and leading a meaningful life (White, 2022). This model, designed to help individuals confront challenges and improve their well-being, underscores the significance of a variety of poignant themes:

- **Positive Emotions**: Concentrating on uplifting experiences and feelings to bolster resilience.

- **Social Support**: The importance of supportive connections in building resilience.

- **Meaning in Life**: The search for purpose and significance as a key element of resilience.

- **Coping**: Crafting strategies to effectively handle stress and difficulties.

- **Physical Well-Being**: Keeping up one's physical health to support mental resilience (White, 2022).

I also shared my academic experiences since starting my International Business Management degree program in September 2020, detailing how resilience and communication were integral to my university life. Along the way, I had instinctively been practising and mastering leadership skills without even realising it, so my personal reflection revealed a lot to me. The following are the different leadership styles I realised had become skills I had unknowingly attained:

- **Adaptive Leadership Style at Work**: I became more flexible, open to new methods, and adept at navigating through changes. This is crucial in a professional setting, where adaptability is essential for success (Northouse, 2021).

- **Passionate Leadership**: My passion for my academic modules drove me to excel. Passionate leaders are motivated to make things happen and put in their best effort (Morgan, 2015).

- **Directive Leadership**: I demonstrated this style during group presentations and at work. I emphasised setting clear rules and regulations for myself and my team members. This clarity ensured that everyone, including myself, understood our tasks and responsibilities when working as a group (Northouse, 2021). In the workplace, I extended my leadership style to training new employees. I established clear and logical objectives for learning. By breaking down tasks step by step, I made it easier for new hires to grasp concepts and perform their duties effectively.

- **Participative Leadership**: By inviting others to share their opinions during group presentations and class work, I practised participative leadership. This approach fosters collaboration and creativity (Northouse, 2021).

- **Supportive Leadership**: I supported my peers by encouraging engagement. When a student struggled and asked for support, I provided assistance, creating a positive learning environment (Northouse, 2021).

- **Task-Oriented Leadership**: In both my university studies and my current employment, I emphasise task completion and meeting deadlines. Task-oriented leaders prioritise efficiency and goal achievement (Northouse, 2021).

- **Inclusive Leadership**: My commitment to treating all colleagues fairly and equally demonstrates inclusive leadership. This approach promotes diversity and ensures everyone feels valued (Veli Korkmaz et al., 2022).

In a strange way, this task had been surprisingly rewarding. I learned a lot about myself and developed an understanding of leadership qualities I did not realise I had. My confidence was bolstered by this new look at myself. My steady personal growth throughout my degree had come as a surprise, and I realised that I had transformed from someone who is led by others to a leader myself.

In the second task of my assignment in leadership, I was faced with creating a 'Personal Development Plan for Leadership Skills and Attributes.' The plan would need to include several subheadings:

- **My Development Record**: Here, I documented my past experiences, achievements, and future growth related to leadership.

- **S.W.O.T Analysis**: Referring to this anagram, I would conduct an analysis of my strengths, weaknesses, opportunities, and threats. This would help me to assess my current position and identify areas for improvement.

- **My Development Plan**: Based on the S.W.O.T analysis, I would then outline specific steps to enhance my leadership skills.

- **Commentary on the Development Plan**: I then had to reflect on the feasibility of the plan, and its alignment with my career aspirations.

- **Limitations in Planning**: Finally, I acknowledged potential limitations, such as time constraints, resource availability, and external factors.

Overall, my development plan was dynamic, and my commitment to continuous growth and balance was foundational. My plan contained elements that I would never have even been aware of at the start of my journey. One major part of the plan had been an obvious addition—an advanced ICT course. Now that I had successfully navigated the basics, I had also identified that I was struggling with more complicated programs, such as the 'Business Simulation Game for Executing Business Strategy.' Taking an advanced course would abolish the panic I encountered when faced with new software or extensive use of computers.

Another step in my personal development plan was more of a surprise. I stated that I have the desire to do a part-time master's course—either Diplomacy, International Business and Trade, or Management with International Business. I had truly enjoyed the 'Critical Perspective of Cross-Border Business' lessons, so I wanted to enhance my knowledge in this area, which would potentially open up higher career paths.

A master's degree. Only four years ago I had blown my mind at the thought of a degree, and now here I was, truly aiming for the stars, this time armed with the belief that I could complete a postgraduate course with astounding results. I also believed that I deserved it, after harnessing my resilience and determination and making it into a personal strength. I would prove to everyone who had ever doubted me that I had academic triumph built into me after all. My plan shone and reflected my strength and fearlessness. No matter the challenges, I would persist in fulfilling my goals with an unwavering desire to obtain the incredible.

Finishing with my personal development plan, I felt, was the perfect way to round off the endless hours of studying I had so unwaveringly dedicated myself to over the previous four years. As I proofread my plan, ready to submit it as my final assignment, I was struck by what it symbolised. This was not only the end of my studies, but the start of my future. The words before me were to be my guide, my steps to success. It was the old me and the new me, all on one page. I could see where the Yusra I had been since my GCSE failure would be coming to an end, and the new Yusra was emerging. I had clearly laid out the measures I must take to nurture this evolving version of myself, and come what may, I promised myself I would achieve these goals. I was quietly grateful to whoever had the genius idea to make this our final assignment, allowing us to complete our journey by giving us a deeper understanding of ourselves and our strengths, leaving with a personalised map that would usher us along on our journey to success. A map that would guide us in dark times and, as abba had promised, be the light at the end of the tunnel I had been waiting for. An instruction manual for defeating the odds.

The completion of the final assignment of my course marked the end of my university journey—my final bid for a high grade and a full degree. I submitted my work on April 23rd, 2024, just before the 2 pm deadline. To others, that might seem like mundane information, but to me, it will always be a date and time that sticks in my mind. Something that would be a landmark on the journey of my life. We find that these moments can be positive or negative. I remember the exact time my first child was born, and the time my abba passed away. Each of us has an array of these moments, but it is up to us to harness the strength, determination, and resilience that lies within us, and make our own positive landmarks. We can't just rely on life to deliver these moments, simply hoping that they will come—we have to make a conscious effort to seize opportunities and see challenges through to the end. So, after four years of striving to overcome challenges, committing to my chosen path, and embracing personal growth, I added 2 pm on April 23rd, 2024 to the list of significant monuments in my life.

The blend of relief, pride and anticipation that filled my heart following the submission of my final assignment made the world stand still. I had crossed an academic milestone that I had truly believed would be unattainable for me. The sensation was phenomenal, almost otherworldly. This trance-like feeling stayed with me only briefly before I realised that there was only one thing left for me to do— wait.

My final grade was to be revealed on June 13th, 2024. It seemed so close yet so distant at the same time. There was a time when I would have found myself dwelling on this, but I made a conscious effort to stay calm and trust myself. I had poured my heart and soul into my degree, so failure would be crushing, but I knew that I also needed to have faith in my abilities and the power of my will to succeed. Questions would flutter through my mind repeatedly: *Was it enough? Will I pass? Will my grades reflect my efforts?* Whenever these concerns would pop up, I would answer myself— *yes.* Worries would be replaced with visions of myself at my graduation, smiling for photos and tossing my graduation cap in the air.

This chapter of my life emphasises my journey through overcoming personal and academic challenges using perseverance and determination. From managing stammering to excelling in complex course modules, the narrative underscores the might of tiny changes in mindset and behaviour, as well as the power of persistent effort. The ability to adapt, seek help, and push beyond comfort zones exemplifies the spirit of never surrendering and conquering all odds. Therefore, we must embrace every challenge as an opportunity for growth. The smallest changes in approach and philosophy can lead to significant improvements in any area of life.

Never surrender to difficulties. Instead, face them head-on, look the challenge in the eye, harness resilience, and adopt determination. By delving into our hearts and souls and recognising that we shouldn't yield to challenging situations, we can alter our habits. Instead of declaring ourselves a 'write-off,' or wallowing in the idea that our journey remains at a standstill, we must pick ourselves up and search for the change we need. Transform the tendency to give up easily, while pursuing the tenacity that drives us on-wards. Change might be slow, and habits might not come easily, but perseverance will conquer all. When we adopt this mindset, we not only build resilience, but also cultivate inner strength, and empower ourselves to overcome obsta-cles fearlessly.

But for now, waiting for my grades was all I could do.

Chapter References:

Anderson, M.H. and Sun, P.Y. "Reviewing leadership styles: Overlaps and the need for a new 'full-range' theory." *International Journal of Management Reviews*. 19(1) (2015): pp. 76–96. doi:10.1111/ijmr.12082.

Barrington, R. (2024). *What is Mendelow's Matrix and How is it Useful?* Oxford College of Marketing Blog. https://blog.oxfordcollegeofmarketing.com/2018/04/23/what-is-mendelows-matrix-and-how-is-it-useful/.

Batna (2023). *Batna.* Corporate Finance Institute.

Chu, P. (2005) MIT Scale Research Report – Massachusetts Institute of Technology.

Crofton, S. 0. and Dopico, L.G. (January 2007). *Zara-Inditex and the growth of fast fashion.* ResearchGate. https://www.researchgate.net/publication/262048389_Zara-Inditex_and_the_Growth_of_Fast_Fashion.

Hayes, J. (2022). *The Theory and Practice of Change Management,* 6th edition. Red Globe Press.

Hill, C.W.L. (2021). *International Business: Competing in the Global Marketplace*, 13th edition. McGraw Hill.

Leroux, J., Thamhaksa, D. and Yokoi, H. (2007). "Home Sweet Home" – A Controversial Thought? A Case Study of IKEA in Japan.

Mishra, A. et al. (May 2021). *Thomas Kilmann Conflict Model.* Management Weekly. https://managementweekly.org/thomas-kilmann-conflict-resolution-model/.

Model, S. and Lopez, P. (2023). Porter's Diamond Model: An Essential Guide for Global Achievement. *SlideModel.*

Morgan, N. (July 2015). *The Art of Passionate Leadership.* Forbes. *https://www.forbes.com/sites/ellevate/2015/07/08/the-art-of-passionate-leadership/.*

Northouse, P.G. (2021). *Introduction to Leadership: Concepts and Practice*, 5th edition. SAGE Publications, Inc.

Pantano, E. and Pizzi, G. (2020) Forecasting artificial intelligence on online customer assistance: Evidence from Chatbot Patents Analysis, Journal of Retailing and Consumer Services.

Peterson, E.R. and Toland, T. (2023). *The 2023 Kearney Foreign Direct Investment Confidence*

Index®. Kearny. https://www.kearney.com/service/global-business-policy-council/foreign-direct-investment%20 confidence-index/2023-full-report.

Retail Revival in Japan (2024). Story of the Second Try to Make It in Japan - *IKEA Museum*. WordPress på Azure.

Review, H.E. (January 2024). *Japan: Porter's Diamond Model-The Competitive Advantage of*

Nations. Hivelr. https://www.hivelr.com/2024/01/japan-porters-diamond-model-the-competitive-advantage-of-nations/.

Shaw, A.A. (2024). PESTLE Analysis of Japan. *Business Management & Marketing*.

Slack, N. and Brandon-Jones, A. (2019). *Operations Management, 9th Edition*. Pearson.

Sliwka, A. et al. "Transformational leadership for deeper learning: Shaping innovative school practices for enhanced learning." *Journal of Educational Administration*, 62(1) (2023): pp. 103–121. doi:10.1108/jea-03-2023-0049.

Sustainable Development Goals (2024). *World Health Organization*.

Thakur, M. (2023). Green Field Investment: A Quick Glance of Green Field Investment. *EDUCBA*.

The Culture Factor Group (2024). Country Comparison Tool. *Hofstede Insights*.

Universities of Wisconsin. (2023). *An Explanation of the Triple Bottom Line*. UW Extended Campus. https://uwex.wisconsin.edu/stories-news/triple-bottom-line/.

Vas, D. (August 2020) *"Digital transformation in the footwear industry: Assessing the potential of IoT on Portuguese SMEs in the Footwear Industry."* Católica-Lisbon School of Business & Economicshttps://repositorio.ucp.pt/bitstream/10400.14/39774/1/202531171.pdf.

Vego, M. (2015) *On Operational Leadership. Available at: jfq-77_60-69_Vego.*

Veli Korkmaz, A. et al. "About and Beyond Leading Uniqueness and Belongingness: A

Systematic Review of Inclusive Leadership Research." *Human Resource Management Review,* 32(4) (2022): p. 100894. doi:10.1016/j.hrmr.2022.100894.

Waldman, D.A. and O'Reilly, C.A. (2020). *Leadership for Organizations,* 1st Edition. SAGE.

White, C. (2022). Mason's Resilience Model: Transforming Fear & Promoting Well-being. *Center for the Advancement of Wellbeing.*

Whittington, R., Regner, P., Angwin, D., Johnson, G. and Scholes, K. (2021). *Fundamentals of Strategy,* 5th edition. Harlow.

British Business Bank. (2025). *What is ESG? A Guide for Businesses.* British Business Bank. https://www.british-business-bank.co.uk/business-guidance/guidance-articles/sustainability/what-is-esg-a-guide-for-smaller-businesses.

Zhelyazkov, G. (2023). *Agile Supply Chain: Zara Case Study Analysis.* Idea Space. http://idea-space.eu:19001/up/319cc877736053b53fe46efc79a29be6.pdf.

Chapter Six:

Transition

Over a span of four years, I had been pursuing an undergraduate degree in International Business Management at Anglia Ruskin University. Due to COVID-19 restrictions, my journey began with two years of online learning, covering the foundation year and the first year of the degree. When it was finally safe for students to start mingling once more, this was followed by two years of on-campus classes, completing the second and third years of the program. Student life had become the norm for me - the routine, the research, the thrill of a good grade, and the fear of failure. There had never been a dull moment, or a second when I regretted the decision to study.

As I completed each assignment and presentation that formed my final year, my mind was like a swinging pendulum, flitting back and forth between the relief that I had completed each module successfully, and the fear that it would not be enough to gain a grade that would allow me to pass. After all, my life had already been somewhat remarkable, particularly raising six thriving children with six very bold personalities, and all of the battles that came with it. When the time had come to enter the next phase of my life, stepping out of the household role that I had always

known and into the business world, I had been totally unaware that my full-time role in sales would eventually lead to
the pursuit of a degree. When this opportunity presented
itself, entirely unexpectedly, I had been hesitant at first.
Becoming a mature student simultaneously with full-time
work seemed like something I wouldn't be capable of. Yet,
something deep within me eagerly embraced the prospect,
driving me to pursue what my better judgement deemed
the impossible. As it turned out, that 'better judgement'
had simply been a lack of self-confidence, something that
I would need to break free from.

As I sit on my living room sofa, following my usual routine, I find myself reminiscing about the past. I recall the
woman who had changed my life that day at the job agency
offices, her eager face encouraging me to apply for a degree despite my CV showing nothing but two GCSEs and
a limited work history. I also recall my initial mistrust, my
low views of myself jumping to doubt her sincerity, wonder-
ing if she was making fun of me. But now, it brings a smile
to my face, remembering the rush of excitement and fear
that I was struck with when my application was accepted.
It felt like the start of a movie—something too good to be
true, that could go terribly wrong at any turn but kept the
characters dancing through the ups and downs, waiting to
see if it would end with a 'happily ever after.' Year after year,
I persevered, finally completing my degree, but I am still
waiting for that happy ending. The wait will soon be over,

and results day is fast approaching, but for now, all I can do is hope and trust in my abilities at long last. I felt the urge to call the agency and thank them for so significantly changing my life, simply by seeing in me something that I had never imagined was there, but I decided that it would be best to wait until my final results were declared. Telling them I had passed would be even more exciting, so I hold onto the hope that I could share good news with them.

During my academic journey, I discovered qualities that I had never known I possessed. Determination. Resilience. Willpower. I had repeatedly gone above and beyond in every module, enduring many knocks along the way, yet resolved to pass and excel. This was a once-in-a-lifetime opportunity for me. I was certain that no other university would consider me a suitable candidate for a course, given that I had such a poor record of results from my previous academic struggles.

Now, having received results for all but two of my completed modules over the four years, I eagerly await the outcomes of my final two: 'Critical Perspective on Cross-Border Business,' and 'Undergraduate Major Project – Leadership in Practice.' These are the results that will determine whether I've successfully completed my degree, or whether I will be met with crushing disappointment, and the anticipation sits heavily in my stomach. The results day is set just a few weeks from now, on June 13th, 2024, with the graduation day waiting for victors, like a monumental embrace of the start of their new lives, just over the horizon, on July 29th.

My life has undergone a significant shift. I have been many different versions of myself over the years. Yusra the academic failure. Yusra the mother and homemaker. Yusra the salesperson and the student. But will I finally become Yusra the graduate? In the days since handing in my final piece of work for my degree, I have found myself in limbo. The anticipation of my final results keeps me on edge, yet I grapple with boredom and restlessness. Where my free time had once been replaced with studies, research and coursework, it now revolves around sitting at home, watching television, and pondering what lies ahead. Occasionally my children encourage me to step outside, inviting me for walks—a gentle reminder that there is much more to my life than my studies, and that even if I have failed, I still have so much to be thankful for. Despite their love and support, I still find myself dwelling on the upcoming results and reminiscing about my days as a student, fixed in a limbo of wistfulness and the impending potential disappointment. This is why I have taken another bold move - to write my memoir. I have been pouring my experiences and academic journey onto these pages, allowing me to relive every part of the roller coaster ride I have just stepped off. Though the question remains—what will results day reveal? —I am also finding comfort in remembering the successes of the last four years. I often wonder what my university classmates are doing. Perhaps basking in holiday bliss, or maybe finding themselves in the same state of purgatory I am in. I hope, for their sakes, that it is not the latter.

However, a recent memory surfaces: my brother's birthday celebration at a Turkish restaurant, just days before submitting my last university assignment.

Gathered alongside my children, siblings, mother, nieces, and nephews, we relished grilled mixed platters and exotic desserts. Gatherings with my large family often raise my spirits, evoking a festival-like atmosphere full of laughs and group photos. For my family, such gatherings reach a headcount of about thirty-five, reminding me how full of joy my life really is, even without a degree. I strive to make them proud, to show them my transformation and, hopefully, see another big gathering with them as we celebrate my graduation. Hopefully.

This May has been quite turbulent, not only in my mind but with the famous British weather, starting the month with a chill, then with a blazing sun, and then a monotonous downpour. My gardening plans have been replaced with my rediscovered love of writing, something I had completely forgotten about until recently. With genuine enthusiasm, I have embraced this new use of my time and have embarked on crafting a book that captures the tapestry of my life experiences—the triumphs and the trials alike. These chapters, mixing my university studies with cherished childhood memories and personal battles, are what emphasise to me the ability I have to overcome life's dips and swerves.

As I find myself reflecting on my educational journey, I am most excited by the content from my last two degree modules: 'Critical Perspective on Cross-Border Business,' and 'The Undergraduate Major Project – Leadership in Practice.' These modules have unveiled latent strengths within me, providing valuable insights, and shaping my understanding of global business dynamics and effective leadership practices. I know that even if my results are a disappointment, I have still learned enough to assist me in a business environment, so I try to keep that in mind. Over the course of my studies, I also uncovered so many personal qualities that I did not expect, as well as learned ways to overcome hurdles and adversaries. I know for a fact that I am not the same woman who first embarked on this journey. And, as always, I am accompanied by abba's wisdom— "After darkness, the light will come."

When I faced losing my job during the COVID-19 pandemic, like many, my life changed. Previously, my main focus had still been on raising my children and ensuring that they received the best education possible, from school to university. My daily routine involved waking up at 5:30 am to cook a curry and a rice dish so that my family had food while I was at work. I would then get ready for work and be out of the door by 8 am. I would have to complete a full day of work to return home and cook once more before helping the children with their homework and heading to bed. It was the same every day, and though I felt relatively fulfilled, I realise now that I am capable of more. The changes that COVID-19 brought to the work life of many saw me working mostly from home, able to complete my household and parenting duties with room left for studies and assignments. A silver lining to be found amongst the global grief. Recovering from the trauma that swept the world during that time had not been easy for anyone, and for some, that recovery is still ongoing, so I am constantly appreciative of the opportunities that university studies brought with them—not simply the potential of a brighter future, but the promise of a more fulfilling present.

One day this May, following a day of work, I settled into a familiar chair, where I had engaged with customers and conducted sales. My son came over, inquisitive about dinner arrangements. A distant memory surged, transporting me to a pre-marriage era when my abba had prohibited me from entering the kitchen. His words resonated: "My dear, you don't need to help in the kitchen, you might burn your hands. Leave it to me—I'll take care of everything." Abba had always treated me with utmost care, constantly assuring me: "Fear not. I'm right here beside you."

These musings led me to consider how the world demanded my initiative. Though abba persistently volunteered to handle tasks on my behalf, he also encouraged me to be more than someone whose life revolved around others. He held a unique role in my life, and his profound understanding and unwavering support remain unparalleled. Life's lessons often reveal that everything comes with a price, and most interactions involve expectations of reciprocity. Yet, my abba's love defied this norm—he gave without seeking anything in return. I hope that my parenting style reflects his. I want my children to be free and confident to pursue their own adventures, and I strive to provide for them, but now that they have reached an age where they can achieve more independence, I am also free to pursue mine. As a mature student, I've observed the world closely, recognising my fortune in having a role model like my abba. Not everybody is fortunate to have such a father, and not every father can embody his unique qualities. And then, there was a cold February day in 2018, when during one of my visits, I mentioned that I had taken the bus and a train to reach him because my car was in the garage for repairs. His immediate response surprised me: "I'll lend you some money to buy a new car!" he exclaimed. Despite his humble beginnings, lack of access to education, and a lifetime of low-paid work, he was always looking out for someone else.

His concern for my comfort touched my heart, but I declined. I explained that I enjoyed the train and bus rides—how they allowed me to watch the world, to feel connected. I urged him to keep the money for himself, to indulge in something he loved. Reflecting on those memories, I am sometimes overcome with emotion. It's evident that when abba learned about my struggles, he couldn't bear it. Even as an adult, he was still watching over me, providing what he could to keep me free of fret. I often remember when I arrived in the UK in 1981, when out for one of our countless walks, he shared with me that he had never bought any of his favourite fruits because of the knowledge that I was still in Bangladesh, unable to access these delights. He had told me that he had been waiting for us to be reunited in the UK because sharing the fruits together would make them all the sweeter. That statement alone is a testament to the unconditional love he had for me, a love so profound that he gave up his favourite fruits just because I wasn't there to enjoy them with him.

My abba's love is irreplaceable, and for me, it remains an unchanging truth. Of course, he loved all his children equally, and we all have different experiences of his love for us, but my time with him made me feel like the most cherished person in the world. As a child, I would playfully ask him whether he would ever leave us, and he would smile and respond, "Where could I possibly go in this world without all of you, my dear children?" This phrase, which I heard from him since childhood, remains unforgettable. No one is as close to me as my *abba* was, in his own way. Some people are not meant to be replaced.

Other memories weigh more heavily on my heart, especially those from the last two days before my abba's passing. On a Saturday morning at exactly 11 am, I said goodbye to my abba as I left one of my regular visits with him. Within fifteen hours, my world turned upside down. He was hospitalised with sepsis and a heart attack.

He was rushed into emergency surgery and though it was successful, the next twenty-four hours remained critical. However, surgery was not enough, and he suffered another heart attack, this time fatal. The moment I heard those words will haunt me until my own final days. The abruptness of the tragedy left me hollow, knowing that he was no longer with me seemed an impossible truth. I deeply desire an alternate reality where I could recount my university experiences to him, especially the myriad of challenges I encountered over those four years, and how I triumphed over each obstacle. I long to share the anticipation of my results with him and find myself frequently reaching into my memories for his many words of support, attempting to apply them to my current situation, and take comfort in them. While I know that others celebrate my achievements, I acknowledge that my abba's pride and emotions would have been exceptionally deep. I have, however, also recently realised that though society often requires parents to be proud of their children, or for children to make their parents proud, the support from my own children during my studies has shown that the opposite is also true. Children can likewise be proud of their parents, as I am of my dear abba, and I learned that my own children are proud of me and my persistent battle to better myself and guide them along the way.

At different times in my life, I've encountered various accounts of mental health challenges, including anxiety disorders, panic attacks, and postnatal depression. I tried to sweep them under the rug, to not allow them to impact my life, but the effects of mental health problems are inevitable. I didn't want to be associated with the stigma, or to have my children feel the repercussions, but in hindsight, this was not an effective way to handle them. My consistently busy lifestyle played a crucial role in this avoidance. Since childhood, I immersed myself in learning about various subjects, striving to be the best I could be, and adapting to my environment. As the eldest of nine siblings, I naturally shouldered significant responsibilities. Caring for my brothers and sisters, interpreting for my parents, and doing what I could to help my family. I never saw these responsibilities as a burden, but they certainly formed who I am today. When I married at twenty years old, I became engrossed in motherhood, raising my own children and pouring my love and energy into their wellbeing. Reflecting on this, I've concluded that my perpetual busyness eventually became a coping mechanism, helping to shield me from my mental health problems, taking control.

After my *abba's* passing, I found myself grappling with mental health issues again, with a new type of depression, much different than the postnatal depression I had battled before. At least that old depression had signified the start of a new life, and the sacrifices I had made to provide it. This new depression signified the end of a life, which had no silver lining. The loss hit me hard, and the pain of his absence was overwhelming. Grief clawed at my heart and rattled my dreams. Life suddenly seemed so much darker without his light and his smile. I tried to tell myself that I should count myself lucky, that some people may not grasp the significance of such heartache because they had never received that much love. But ultimately, the pain of losing someone you've loved your whole life is hard to forget. I couldn't easily accept that he was gone—no longer there to talk to, no longer a presence in our family home.

About three months after his death, I began experiencing physical symptoms. A heavy sensation settled on the left side of my chest, accompanied by persistent pain. Alarmed, I sought medical advice. The doctor's diagnosis was something I had not thought possible. The grief had manifested itself physically, causing anxiety, panic attacks, and this gnawing pain. They advised me to redirect my thoughts away from my loss, focusing on positive aspects of life instead, finding joy in the things I still had, and embracing good things when they came my way. Despite delving into my abba's proverbs to find coping strategies for my grief, I discovered that it's an incredibly difficult challenge. Something much easier in theory than it is in practice. Even though I could look back on previous advice and try to recycle the wise words that he spoke, it took patience and practice to even begin to heal.

My main diversion was to focus on my children, reminding myself that I needed to be strong, happy, and healthy for their sake. This mindset served as a mechanism to ease the discomfort when memories of my *abba* flooded my thoughts, focusing on the new generation more than mourning the loss of the older one. By that time, my youngest child was already a teenager, and naturally, the intensity of the care they needed from me was less than it once was. They no longer needed me to hold their hands on the walk to school or keep a watchful eye on them as they played.

Nevertheless, their presence was a reminder of the good I had in my life, and the achievements I had made as a mother. It has been six years since my abba passed, and the loss still grips me, I know that I will never get over the pain of losing him, but I also know that he would be proud of the woman I am, and the work it has taken me to get here. Pursuing my degree during the COVID-19 pandemic— from the foundation year to the final year—has been unexpectedly helpful in easing the pain and grief of losing my abba. Overcoming the challenges posed by each module has provided a sense of purpose and distraction, forcing me to address my low self-esteem and anxiety. I was also in a position where I needed to prove myself, and the ugly truth of my avoidance raised its head. I realised that my anxiety and lack of self-confidence would need to be tackled in order to succeed. I had to quickly learn how to counter the deep-rooted impact my mental health was having in order to not jeopardise my degree. It wasn't easy, and it played a major role in my life as a student, but it also made me recognise and appreciate my resilience all the more.

Facing the anxieties of the unknown, and grappling with the fear of public speaking, could have hindered me during my studies, but facing these issues head-on was the only option. I have noted that I could not have completed my studies if I had not developed an understanding of the way my brain works and handles certain scenarios.

Whenever I encountered life's difficult challenges, I always had one of my abba's little sayings or quotes that I could apply to the situation. One particular adage he often repeated when I complained about tough times after marriage was as follows: "Breaking a home is easy—just dismantle all the bricks. But rebuilding that home to its original state, with all its decorations, can take a lifetime." His wisdom emphasised the importance of deep thinking, maintaining a calm mindset, and seeking alternative solutions to secure long-term well-being. Of course, this proverb of his isn't just applicable to home life - it echoes the truth in the value of not giving up. These particular words have given me the strength to endure the toughest situations. September 1st, 2024 will mark my thirtieth wedding anniversary. Like all partnerships, we have faced our ups and downs, but the success of these thirty years has embodied hard work, dedication, and the ability to work through rocky patches or disagreements. I know full well that we have both fallen back on abba's wisdom at times, and that has allowed us to thrive.

I encourage everyone to embrace my abba's teachings. The understanding of his guidance can lead us through challenges, conquer hardships and emerge victorious. These teachings have profoundly shaped my character, and rediscovering the truth in them has been a powerful part of my journey these past four years.

Regardless of the nature of the challenges we face, the words still ring true. Welcoming understanding of these words into our hearts can provide us with a significant advantage in life, giving us strength, and the ability to hold on to hope.

One of his key lessons, as I have mentioned before, is, "Be patient. After hardship, light will show," which aligns with our Islamic belief in the Quran, Chapter 2, Verse 153: "Allah is with those who are patient." This verse emphasises that patience is essential to persevere through hardship or loss. Another verse that resonates with my name, Yusra, which means 'ease,' is from Chapter 94, Verse 6: "Undoubtedly, along with hardship there is ease." This verse conveys that in every difficult situation, there is always something to be grateful for. With hardship, *Allah* also gives us the strength and patience to bear it. It signifies hope and comfort, urging us not to give up under stress, as ease will eventually come.

These verses have provided me with support, strength, and the willpower to remain patient and conquer any challenges, no matter what they may be. I acknowledge that not everyone will believe in a god or be of a specific faith, but this does not make the teachings inapplicable. Faith can be in oneself, in those around us, or in the possibility of better things, but ultimately, faith is important. And, as we use faith to keep us going through life, we develop wisdom of our own to nurture and pass on.

On a recent sunny afternoon, I decided to explore a local park in London. The park, adorned with a serene lake, welcomed me with open arms. As I approached the entrance, my eyes fell upon an ice cream van, its colourful exterior beckoning me. Unable to resist, I indulged in my favourite vanilla ice cream, savouring the cold, creamy delight. The taste of childhood summers. With each lick, I felt the world melt away, replaced by a sweetness that I relished as I strolled through the park. It felt almost metaphorical, reminding me that even at these times of great unease for me, there is still joy to be found in the little things.

The park stretched out in front of me like an artist's canvas. A flock of birds, gathered on the grass, seemed to hold a secret council. I imagined that perhaps they debated the day's affairs, or simply revelled in the sun's warmth, or maybe they awaited a kind soul to offer them a morsel of food. I felt a wave of wonder, the sudden appreciation of the myriad of life that surrounds us, unacknowledged, yet adding to the ambience of the world with twitters and their own little experiences. It can be so easy to overlook the things around us, taking them for granted or underappreciating their contributions, especially when we are distracted by our own troubles, but there is beauty in everything, just waiting to be seen.

Walking a little further, I was greeted by a grand oak tree, its branches reaching skyward. The wind, a mischievous companion, tousled its leaves, making them dance in the breeze as though they were celebrating the gentle sun. The rich shades of green and sturdy boughs were no doubt the home to an array of wildlife, living in unison, yet different in every way. It stood there, a firm sentinel of time, boldly reminding me that there are things in the world so much bigger and wiser than I.

As I strolled onward, I reached a lake, calm and shimmering. Ducks glided across its surface, sending gentle ripples across the mirrored sky. I knew that they would be paddling like crazy below the water in order to propel them to whatever destination they were pursuing. I understood from my own experience how this reflected ourselves, and the efforts we must put into reaching our goals, no matter how easy it may look to others. But I also saw more than a lake. I saw a thing of beauty, welcoming the lives of others, letting them dance across its surface, supporting their existence without a complaint. This made me think of motherhood, the perfect analogy, the ease with which we can accept our role in nurturing the life around us, despite the ripples and frantic paddling.

My gaze lifted, tracing the horizon. The boundless blue sky stretched infinitely, adorned with fluffy white clouds. In the distance, a vibrant funfair came into view, its colourful attractions and dancing rides. Parents accompanied their children, watching as they fizzed with excitement. Memories stirred—a carousel of yesteryears. I recalled my abba, strong and gentle, lifting me onto his shoulders at a bustling funfair. Shared laughter, cotton candy, and dizzying rides—they all danced in my mind. These memories were bittersweet, triggering a lump in my throat as the reminder of my loss jumped back into my mind, but I was hit by a profound realisation. The children I saw before me, skipping along by their parents' side, grinning ear-to-ear, revealing their missing teeth or endearing dimples—they were making memories, too. These would be moments that they would also cherish, wherever the tangles of life's journey may take them. I was grateful for these memories, despite the sorrow that came attached, and I was grateful that this new generation would also have them to bring them comfort at times of sorrow, too. A feeling of sonder washed over me, recognising the intricacies of the lives unfolding all around me, somehow making the jolly music and swirling lights of the funfair all the more joyous.

In that moment, I shed my worries and my identity, becoming one with the simple wonders around me. The birds sang, the ducks glided and squabbled, and I swayed to their rhythm. I had never felt quite so peaceful. The anxieties about my results and my desire for closure took a brief hiatus from my thoughts as the gentle breeze caressed my skin, and I wished that this idyllic weather could last forever, so that the serenity of the park would remain. I took a deep breath, letting the freshness of the air fill my lungs. I came to realise that I now see the world from an entirely different perspective. Education has empowered me. Reclaiming my fortitude has been a rekindling of my spirit. Every phase of my life has been as rich with growth as it has with hardships. Focusing on defeating our battles is of benefit, but keeping focus on our simple blessings can make the battle easier to cope with.

Eventually, and with great consideration, I have decided to undertake an online non-fiction writing course. I had become restless with the lack of challenge my life suddenly held since ending my degree. The end of classes had left me with spare time that I did not know how to fill, and I realised that I needed a new adventure to embark upon, a new expansion of knowledge. I was also aware that it would be a welcome distraction from what felt like an eternity of waiting for the results of my degree to come to fruition. As my epiphany in the park had shown me, there was so much more to life than dwelling on something out of our control, and I intended to continue my exploration of this. I would spend two hours every Thursday evening delving into the intricacies of non-fiction pieces, knowing that it would ultimately serve to enhance the memoir I have taken up writing. The reignition of my passion for writing was first sparked during the final year of my degree, where the extensive written assignments saw me reclaim the hobby I enjoyed in my school years, and had long since forgotten. I wanted to explore and understand non-fiction creative writing, which has its own unique rules and distinct beauty in styles. The course had a variety of aspects, all of which I thoroughly enjoyed, but one particularly enjoyable element was to interview a classmate in my course.

My classmate shared a significant transition period in her life with me, one that had me inspired. Learning about others and their journeys through life can be a valuable tool for understanding our own lives. We can take comfort and motivation from the experiences of other people, and in this instance, I was enthralled by her story. In 1987, she embarked on a journey to Ouagadougou, the capital of Burkina Faso in West Africa, with the purpose of reuniting with her boyfriend, who was already working in the city. However, upon landing, she was greeted by a startling scene - the airport swarmed with military personnel, their guns at the ready. She told me that the tension in the air was palpable, and her mind raced with questions to which she had no answers. As she observed her surroundings, she noticed young soldiers, some dressed in military uniforms, others simply wearing jeans and T- shirts. Their weapons and machinery created a cacophony of noise, accompanied by the chaos of people shouting and screaming.

I delved into her experience more, hoping to find the answers that she had not found at the time. I unearthed a significant historical event: In 1987, Ouagadougou, Burkina Faso, witnessed a significant historical clash between two powerful figures— Thomas Sankara and Blaise Compaore. Their friendship had blossomed during military training sessions in Morocco, many years before. However, Sankara, serving as prime minister, championed the August Revolution, advocating for progressive policies and social justice. Blaise, once a trusted ally, harboured divergent ambitions. In a meticulously arranged scheme, he betrayed Sankara, orchestrating his assassination and seizing power, going on to rule for twenty-seven years. The disillusionment of the Burkinabé population culminated in protests, ultimately compelling Blaise's resignation in 2014. Despite evading justice, he was convicted in absentia. Sankara's legacy endures, celebrated by activists worldwide (Abdoulie, 2017).

In a way, the conflict between Thomas Sankara and Blaise Compaore in Burkina Faso made me think of one of my own friendships—a bond forged with a childhood friend since we first met in secondary school. Even today, we remain exceptionally close, and I proudly consider her my best friend. Though currently we reside in different cities in the UK, and pursue distinct professional paths, we remain in constant contact. I have never encouraged, nor would I ever encourage my best friend to enter into a joint venture or work together in the same environment, in similar career paths, especially when it involves financial matters. These dynamics are delicate, and we must tread carefully to avoid clashes. Similarly, I would discourage any blood family members from entering business partnerships or pursuing the same profession as mine. The story of Thomas Sankara and Blaise Compaore serves as a cautionary tale—a trusted friendship that turned into enmity when bringing power and politics into the partnership. To me, this piece of history serves as a valuable lesson: prioritise safeguarding friendships over embarking on uncertain business ventures. It's wiser to explore diverse career paths, strike a balance between partnerships, and cherish genuine connections. Competing with those we love can only result in inevitable heartache. True success transcends wealth, fame, or shortcuts—it lies in celebrating achievements with loved ones rather than pushing them to achieve the same.

On the last day of May 2024, I continued burying myself in my work, ensuring no customer slipped away, and harnessing the fresh knowledge I had been granted on my degree course to constantly improve. As the clock ticked, my mind raced. It would be exactly two weeks until the day I had been waiting for. June 13th marked the official release date of my degree results—the day I had been craving and dreading at the same time. Then, at 2:47 pm, a message arrived in our university group chat: the results were out early. I couldn't focus on work anymore. I needed to know. Heart pounding, I logged into my Anglia Ruskin University student account, trembling as I navigated to the results section. Although the final degree result had not been included, my grades for the last two modules sat waiting for me. In all honesty, I was not relieved. I was dumbfounded and full of doubt. I was certain that there had been some kind of mistake, so I logged out, and then back in, testing for some sort of error and expecting to see the letters on the screen change. The same grades stared back at me. I'd poured my heart and soul into those modules, knowing that they would shape my final degree outcome.

But there they remained. My results. I received 'A' grades for both of my last modules: 'Critical Perspectives on Cross-Border Business,' and 'Undergraduate Major Project (Leadership in Practice).' I had put so much work into these modules, particularly enjoying the 'Cross-Boarder' assignments, and this work had actually paid off. I wanted nothing more than to shout it from the rooftops, but I had to hold in my delight for just that little bit longer, watching the clock tick until the end of the workday so that could I share the news with my loved ones. I decided, however, to keep the information to just a select few. Despite feeling near euphoria, I had to keep my feet on the ground, knowing that the official results were not yet set in stone, as adjustments could easily be made between now and June 13th. However, the wait ended early. Just five days later, I received the news that the official final grades— the cumulation of every module grade—had been released. The second I got a break from work, I logged into my account, fingers shaking as I did so. And it was then that I was met with the words I had been so desperate to see: *"First-Class Honours."*

I was so full of disbelief, the same self-doubt popping up with a wave of nausea. I even called my husband to ask him to double-check. He read it aloud, echoing the results I had been longing to hear. *"First-Class Honours."* I couldn't hold back my emotions, I wept with joy, simply repeating, *"I've done it! I've done it!"* My past failures suddenly felt as though they had been washed away, a tidal wave of achievement cancelling out all the heartache I still carried from those devastating GCSE results.

Later, I shared the news with the rest of my family. Their pride in me bolstered the pride I felt in myself. Their happiness for me filled me to the brim in a way I had never experienced before. This was an achievement that I had attained on my own, not something that had been simply granted to me, like a birthday or an anniversary, so the celebrations felt all the more empowering. I'll admit that internally, I danced with joy for weeks, at times still trying to fully grasp the reality of the situation but unwilling to let that feeling go. I had given every module of the course one hundred per cent effort and that effort was absolutely worth it for this feeling, and the knowledge that I have opened so many new avenues for myself to explore in the future. I had buried myself in my studies to achieve this, taking initiative and tackling my personal shortcomings full-on. My lack of math and I.T. knowledge, as well as my difficulties with presentations had been conquered, and I had proven to everyone just what I was truly capable of. Many times, I had doubted if I belonged there, in that class of forty students, most of whom were much younger than me and well-versed in trends in companies, cars, current affairs, maths, and technology. I had felt like a fraud, watching lesson after lesson as others seemed to sail through their experience.

That said, I also had to remind myself that we never truly know what is going on in another person's life or how their walk through life is unfolding, so comparing ourselves to others is futile. It only serves to do everyone an injustice. Perhaps they were a whizz on a computer but did not have a wise and supporting *Abba* like I had. Maybe they knew a lot more about current market trends than I did but had not got my sales experience. There are numerous ways my life's journey has been different, so as hard as it was to recognise at the time, the point in comparison is nil.

This success had been far from without sacrifice. The extensive research I had done for each assignment, the stress of creating the perfect slides for presentations despite my limitations, the extra support I had had to reach out for, the time missed out on with family and friends, and the lost hours of sleep were the equivalent of my blood, sweat, and tears, poured into this labour of love. Admittedly, there had been a fair share of my own tears thrown into that mix, but all of it had been worth it.

One of the biggest slogs had been the lack of sleep. Balancing my studies with full-time work and being a mother meant that my assignments would often see me staying up until three, sometimes even four in the morning, making every minute count, as I strived to meet deadlines. After just a few hours of sleep, I would have to be ready to start work at 8:30 am, forcing myself to run on fumes. It was challenging, but I had to accept and adapt to this routine if I were to succeed. As a mother, however, I had already had my fair share of experience of running on very little sleep. I had six children, all born within ten years, so naturally, at that time sleep became a distant memory. I was constantly on my feet, staying at home to raise my energetic gaggle of children with broken sleep at night, as they cried for feeds or attention.

With each new child, it felt like peaceful sleep was never going to come to me. From night feeds, they grew to waking me because of nightmares or fevers or any manner of the needs a small child has of their mother. I eventually adapted to and accepted this new reality. I had my first child at twenty-one and my sixth at thirty-one. Perhaps being so young had given me more strength to survive with so little sleep back in those days, because this time round it had been so much more challenging. I think it is important for all parents to pause and praise themselves for the power they have inside them when making these sacrifices, but it is also important for us to remember to offer ourselves kindness and to know that we also have the ability to make our children proud. It can feel very lonely sometimes.

Friends can fall by the wayside and relationships can become strained. Sometimes I felt helplessly alone, as if my only adult interactions were with my children's teachers or phone calls with my parents, but in reality, I was not alone. I had six beautiful, brilliant children to watch grow and thrive, knowing that it had been my hard work and sacrifice that saw them become adults themselves.

Often in life, we aim to keep our past behind us and try to forget about the tough times, but reflecting on and remembering these times makes us stronger and gives us the willpower to improve. Reflection has helped me correct mistakes, change old habits, form new ones, and seek new directions to achieve success. It has assisted me in building greater resilience and perseverance, without surrendering. I would like to emphasise to everyone the power of embracing reflection, learning from mistakes, changing, and adapting. Looking behind you can help you as you seek new directions and build strength, moving forward. Owning these hardships and cherishing them as a lesson rather than a loss is what helps us to never surrender and shows us how to turn past challenges into stepping stones for future success.

My family celebrated my results for a week, but internally, I am still celebrating. In fact, I think that this is something I will be privately celebrating for a long time. My family's pride in me, especially that coming from my children, has been stunning, but the pride I now feel in myself and the fresh outlook in life I have obtained during my journey feels the most rewarding. The only pride I am missing is my abba.

According to our 'Islamic Hadith,' which provides religious law and guidance, everything comes to a halt for the deceased after their death. The most valuable legacy they leave behind includes ongoing charity, beneficial knowledge they have imparted, or a righteous child who will pray for them and give charity on their behalf. For being my abba, for raising me, for loving me and providing every comfort, for being the family's breadwinner, for his limitless support in my life, and for shaping me into who I am today, I pray to Allah (God) to grant my abba the gardens of peace. Ameen.

Recently, someone who is soon to turn fifty asked me what it was like for me when I reached that milestone. I replied, "It all depends on what I've achieved by this age." They seemed puzzled by my response. In the run-up to my fiftieth birthday, I had felt terrible. It seemed to me that a person who had lived for half a century should have so much more to show for it. Of course, my wonderful children were testament enough, in reality, but I was ashamed of my lack of education and life experience. Most people my age seemed so much more interesting or adventurous or had lives rich with anecdotes to share at parties. Now, I reflect on those words. I have a fulfilling marriage of almost thirty years, I have six brilliant and beautiful children, and I have a degree. Sure, I could have done things the other way around, like most do—a degree first, then a career, then marriage and kids—but I realised that it isn't the path to the destination that counts, or the speed at which you travel, but the knowledge you gain along the way. I have achieved so much.

These achievements, despite being in such different areas, are all equal. I am proud of sticking through tough times to maintain my marriage. Proud of each of my children and my ability to fill their lives with love and support as they pursue their dreams. And I am proud that I hold First-Class Honours in my degree. Each of these achievements has required a lot of strength and spirit, day after day, giving it my all. Every night awake with a teething baby, and every night awake cramming my studies. Every challenging teenage tantrum and every challenging assignment. Parenthood is not for the fainthearted. Neither is being a student.

Ultimately, the most rewarding things in my life have been the most difficult to achieve. So, when I replied, "It all depends on what I've achieved by this age." the meaning was simple - it doesn't matter your age, nor the path you have taken, it just matters that you strive to achieve, in whatever form that comes. Age, setbacks, and obstacles are not barriers but stepping stones to your dreams. Whether your challenges are big or small, you can always start fresh and chase your desires, as you do have the power to overcome them. Embrace your journey with courage and determination, and you'll discover that the impossible is within your grasp. Hold your difficulties as something to cherish, as these are things that form you and give you wisdom to pass on to others. As I treasure my abba's advice, be someone who has advice to share with those around you, whether it be your children, your friends, or even just someone you met at a party who happens to feel adrift. Life is about achievements, and for some, simply surviving is an achievement in itself. Whatever form your achievements come in, use them, and the battles that came with them, to leave something good in the lives of others.

Looking to my future, past my graduation at the end of this coming July, I have already decided what the next chapter of my life will be. Though initially I considered undertaking a master's degree called 'Diplomacy, International Business and Trade,' I have set my eyes on another venture. My degree will open many doors for me and will undoubtedly allow me to climb to new heights in a business-based career, yet I have surprised myself with a new goal. It had always been a desire of mine to further my education, despite writing it off as impossible at such an early age, so I will do so, just in a different field. I have decided to pursue an MA in creative writing. There are no limits in life. Sometimes, we may think that life is taking us in one direction, but it is perfectly okay to change your mind and take a different route. We must be willing to make changes, stay strong in our goals, and work towards our short-term and long-term visions. Dedication and planning are key, but looking into personal development and growth should never end.

The possibility of pursuing a master's in international business is still at the back of my mind, but for now, I am happy for that to wait. It is never too late, perhaps that will be a venture in the future, but only time will tell. For now, I am going with my heart. Though thoroughly unexpected, the enjoyment I got from the written assignments during my studies and the discovery of my natural ability left me feeling inspired. Of course, I would have to continue my full-time work in order to support my family and maintain my chances of progressing up the career ladder, which limited my options when it came to which universities I could apply for. In the end, I chose Hull University. Their classes will be entirely online and those that are held during office hours can be repeated on evenings or on weekends. It feels like the perfect fit, and a challenge I am eager to face.

As I stand at the threshold of a new chapter in my life, it is important to honour the chapters that came before. I need to be proud of the child who left the country of her birth and integrated into an alien society. I need to be kind to the teenager who was so heartbroken at her failed GCSEs. I need to admire the dedicated mother and wife who faced the endless trials of raising six children. I need to acknowledge the boldness of the woman who entered the workforce for the first time, despite her lack of experience. And right now, I am celebrating the graduate, who fought tooth and nail to achieve First-Class Honours as a mature student. I am grateful for every tear shed and sleepless night that those chapters saw, as I know that they will see me through the chapters that are to come. I also need to have gratitude for the privileges I have had along the way—a loving abba, a supportive family, healthy children, and a resilience that I was not even aware that I had. While the future remains uncertain, I am ready to embrace new opportunities with the same determination that has guided me thus far.

While I wait for graduation day to arrive, I am also preparing to conquer the MA in Creative Writing over the next two years. I am ready to face all the new challenges this program will bring, and just like with my undergraduate degree, I will give my very all to overcome any difficulties that come my way. After all, education never ends.

Chapter Reference:

Abdoulie, S. "The chronology of military coup d'états and regimes in Burkina Faso: 1980-2015."

Milletleraras, 48(0) (2017): pp. 1–18. doi:10.1501/ intrel_0000000310.

Chapter Seven:

Graduation

As I prepare for graduation day tomorrow, I have found myself in a strange limbo.

Over the past few months, I have been busying myself by writing this book. I have used my spare time to pour my thoughts, feelings, and memories into the pages, hoping to capture the meandering path my degree in international business has taken me. The unforeseen twists and turns my life has faced in recent years have been intense, but the personal growth and new potential that has come with it are invaluable. I recognised that the time I poured into the degree left me very little time for self-reflection, so taking the realisations and emotions and sharing them in writing has been somewhat cathartic. In all honesty, I thought that this piece would come to an end when I received my results, but I realised that this was not the case—that the show isn't over until the fat lady sings, as they say. I am sitting on the eve of one of the most significant days of my life - my graduation.

The excitement I feel is shared, which makes it all the more rich. My household has been buzzing for a few days now-my children, my husband, my mother, my siblings—all beaming at me with new pride in their eyes. Being proud of myself is one thing, but in reality, it is not even the main thing I had set out to achieve. All I had set out to attain was a job. Seizing the opportunity for a degree had come next, knowing that it would unlock potential career paths at some point in the future. This bubbling feeling of fulfilment was not what I had expected to come with it. But to share this with my family has been a bonus that has doubled my sense of self-worth and achievement.

"Ma!" my children keep saying. "We knew you could do it!"

"My love." My husband smiles. "Please recognise how far you have come!" "My daughter—you make us so proud!" my amma keeps phoning to share.

"The graduate!" I long to hear my abba exclaim. "The one who has conquered the odds. The child who has grown to show the world what tenacity looks like. The woman who has proven that the light is there, waiting beyond the hardships. My śiśu. My Yusra." I can close my eyes and imagine his voice, joining the beautiful words I hear from my family. Knowing that despite his painful absence, I carry his pride within me.

Maybe some would think this pride is self-serving or vain, but the reality is that we should always take pride in our achievements. Pride is proof of growth. An understanding of the mountains we have climbed to get to where we stand. The acknowledgement of our hardships, and understanding of our power to overcome them, is indispensable, and will propel us past the next battles life may throw our way.

Relish your achievements, because they are a well-earned result of your willpower, your resilience, and your journey. Pride is not something to be ashamed of, it is something to be grateful for, but overall, it is something that proves your inner strength. So, rejoice in it.

I went to bed hours ago, but instead of sleep, I have been met with an itching excitement, tossing and turning with a mind full of thoughts. Hence why I am here, late at night, adding another chapter to my story, despite knowing that tomorrow will bring an early rise, a busy day, and a flurry of emotions. Along with the excitement, I found myself reminiscing about the three graduations I've already attended: my eldest and second brothers' graduations, and my second child's graduation.

Graduation ceremonies have limits to the number of guests a graduate can bring. That's probably a good thing, since there would be no room for all of the people wanting to cheer for their loved ones as they collected that esteemed scroll. I recognise how blessed I am to have so many people to select from. Back then, I was sitting with the other guests who were there to beam as their loved ones took to the stage, bowing and shaking hands with high-ranking academic officials and dignitaries. But this time, it will be different. This time it will be me, making my family beam and cheer as I take my long-awaited turn.

Two days ago, I met with the women of my life—our own little celebration of the journey I have taken. Together, at a charming Turkish restaurant in the heart of East London, we shared food, stories, and memories until late in the evening. I looked at my sisters, daughters, and sisters-in-law, realising that this kind of kinship is something I am lucky to have, and to treasure it immeasurably.

As women, and Muslims, we walk an extraordinary path - a unique experience of life that is filled with unique experiences and inherent challenges. I cherish my identity, culture, and religion, and it never feels like a burden, but it is something that isn't always easy. Like any minority, there are automatic setbacks. Simply by being a woman, we walk a different path to men. Being Muslim offers a distinct experience compared to other faiths or belief systems. We must accept the reality of life, our identity, our roots, and the purpose Allah has created for us. Above all, I believe in being grateful and happy for the life Allah has given me.

Diversity is what makes life rich, but it is not without challenges. It is important, whoever we are, to know that the things that make us different are the things that make our journey special. Every journey has a unique starting point, an exclusive set of obstacles, adversities, and falls, but the key is to own that.

As I watched the women of my life filled with joy on my behalf, I appreciated their journeys, too. The similarities and differences between us, the things that bring us together.

So, I find myself urging anyone reading this to embrace their identity, find comfort in those similar to you, and celebrate the differences of those who are not.

My adulthood started on a path traditional for my cultural heritage—marrying at twenty, raising children, and following the path that I thought was already carved out for me, solidified by the GCSE failures that had stood in my way. I do not regret that choice, and it was made freely, but I have also come to understand that my experiences as a woman, a mother, and a Muslim, just like the women around the table with me, are not the only part of my identity. Be proud of who you are, where you come from, and of your heritage, whatever these things may be. Celebrate these things about yourself. But also know that your life is your own. Pursuing new things does not take anything away from your identity, it merely adds to your rich and precious life.

Tomorrow will add another token to my identity, and I find myself impatient to claim it. Despite this eagerness, I also find a layer of inner peace. There is a huge part of me that has grown during my university studies. Not only have I filled my brain with knowledge that will open new doors, but I have filled my heart with courage. That tomboyish spirit that saw me following my dreams during my childhood has returned. There is a new boldness in my character that proves my evolution. A whole new world has opened up for me, beckoning adventures and the unknown. I could not have imagined, all those years ago, when I simply wanted a job, that I would be here, waiting for the dawn to bring a day to remember. As I ready myself for a monumental milestone in my life, thoughts racing and anticipation electrifying my mind in the most beautiful way, I look forward to adding a new element to my identity: Graduate.

*****

Finally, those restless nights turned into the day I had been waiting for. July 29th, 2024—my graduation. By 4:30 am, I was already out of bed. Hanging on my wardrobe, ready to wear, was the beautiful new white saree I had chosen for the occasion. I was already itching to get dressed, excited to combine my cultural outfit with the traditional gown and mortarboard worn by graduates.

Attending by my side would be my husband and youngest son. My youngest son, who had so patiently supported me through every bump on the road, every wobble in my confidence, and every evening left to cook his own dinner when I dashed off to class or crammed for tests. He had even donated his time, proofreading my assignments or suggesting improvements in written pieces. When most teenagers his age would probably have been hanging out with their friends or playing computer games, he selflessly offered up his spare time to patiently support me along my journey. He was a big part of my success on this road, and I was proud of him for this—the display of kindness and support he had shown when I had needed it so greatly. He, in turn, had told me how proud he was of me for facing my fears and pushing aside hesitations so that I could fulfil my dream, so sharing this day with him felt fitting. My second son had also so graciously supported me with my struggles during the mathematical elements of my first year, and I count myself blessed to have children with such gracious and giving hearts.

Parents are required to be role models to their children by necessity. We have to lead the way and allow them to follow the paths we take and the qualities we embody in order for them to grow into decent human beings with tuned moral compasses. What is less talked about, however, is the fact that it is possible for them to also grow into our own role models. I made sacrifices throughout my life for them, giving up time with friends or an opportunity for a career in order to raise them, and for them to echo my actions and make sacrifices for me when I needed them proved to me that they had not taken it all for granted, and that they had followed my path. However, at such a young age, their eagerness to help was inspiring, and they made their sacrifices all the greater, as it was not their responsibility to do so. I admire them deeply for the young men they are becoming, and the character they have shown.

Of course, I would have loved for both of my sons to have been able to be there with me. In fact, I would have loved all of my family to be there. But the limit the number of guests graduates could bring wouldn't allow more than two, so we all agreed that my youngest son would be joining me.

Part of the reasoning behind choosing my youngest son was because my second son will already be attending a graduation with me later this year—his own. At the start of September, he is set to graduate with a Bachelor of Science from Goldsmiths University of London, having worked so diligently on his Computer Science course for years. It will be an honour to be there with him as he is rewarded for his efforts. It is a point of particular pride, knowing that I will be graduating the same year as my son. It feels like an alignment of generations as equals. Proof that age is no barrier when it comes to education, that the corny phrase 'it's never too late' is actually true.

We travelled from London to Chelmsford Cathedral, where my graduation was to be held. The journey took about an hour, but it felt much longer. Realistically, this journey had taken over four years. It had begun at the click of a button, sending off my application, fully sure that there was no chance of being accepted into the university course. But somehow, this hour's journey felt even longer. The cathedral was a decadent monument of historical Britain, handsome and proud. I could never have imagined, when I stepped off the plane that cold November forty-three years ago, that I would one day be standing in a place of such beauty, ready to commemorate one of the biggest achievements a wide-eyed child from Bangladesh could dream of. As my husband and son waited with the rest of the guests, I joined the other graduates to don the traditional attire.

The contrast between my dazzling white saree and the deep navy-blue gown and graduation cap brought a lump to my throat. I could see the winding journey of my life represented by the combination of conventions, the garments confirming how far I had come. I felt powerful. I was just like any other student, not even considering my age, the fact that I'm a mother of six, or that I'm fifty years old. I felt equal to all the other students, whether they were my age, ten years younger, or even as young as twenty-one. We had been on this journey together and were about to be rewarded with the honour we had earned.

I looked around to see the faces of my husband and son. As soon as our eyes met, a wave of peace came over me. Although my youngest son is the baby of the family, his optimistic, patient, and calm demeanour reminds me of my abba. The twinkle in his eye and the genuineness of his smile felt as though my abba's pride for me had been passed down to this youngest generation, and that gave me great comfort.

For a while, we milled around the flowerbeds and noble trees that surrounded the cathedral, having our photographs taken and chatting with the other graduates, sharing our thoughts and feelings. I introduced my husband and son to some of my classmates, who had grown to become good friends. People smiled and complimented my saree. I had worried for a moment when we first started mingling, noticing that I was the only person dressed in traditional Muslim attire, but guests and graduates alike were full of admiration, elevating my confidence and sense of belonging. One of my classmates even said she didn't recognise me at first, and that I looked like I was getting married. At one time, I would have been terrified by the thought of getting on stage before a sea of strangers, all eyes on me, but the growth in confidence that the course has granted me had completely diminished these fears, replacing them instead with excitement. I was itching to get on stage and be seen by the world.

As 11 am approached, my son and husband headed to their seats, joining the rest of the guests, excitedly chatting, with a hum that filled the air. I joined my peers, sitting on stage, eager to be standing with the esteemed scroll in my hand. After speeches from various academic officials and Anglia Ruskin University alumni, the host began calling the students one by one to take their place and receive their hard-earned reward. I had to pinch myself, quite literally, awash with disbelief. I could sense that those around me felt the same. After what felt like a lifetime, my name was announced and I strode to the stage, head held high, saree flowing around me, heart pounding in my chest.

People often claim that at the moment someone dies, their life flashes before their eyes, but somehow, I found this happening to me in this moment. My early childhood in Bangladesh, my later childhood in the UK, my heart-broken sobs over my failed GCSE results, my wedding day, the births of my children, the struggles of motherhood, losing my abba, the highs and lows I had met during my studies. Each significant moment along the journey of my life flowed through my mind in an instant, but this was not a death. This was a new beginning. This was the moment I realised that I was truly myself. Yusra, the graduate, standing on stage with a scroll in my hand, proving on paper that I had come further than I could ever have dreamed. I searched the faces in the audience of my husband and son, locking eyes as they clapped their hands.

This moment will be etched in my mind for the rest of my life. The gratitude I have for my family and friends, for their support during this transition, is immeasurable, my pillars of strength during every moment of doubt. I recognise the sacrifices that they, too, had made. My son, who offered his tutelage without complaint when I needed it the most. My friends, who accepted cancelled plans and less time together. My husband, who calmed me when the pressure had me in tears. My abba, who despite no longer physically being with me was still a voice of reason and advice in the back of my mind. It is often said that we get out of life what we put in. Putting in the work, harnessing our resilience, and powering through, even when times are tough, does pay off. It may take years, it may take less, but without taking those steps we cannot move forward. Giving up is simply not an option, though that may often feel like the case. Quitting is doing oneself an injustice - stealing from oneself the joy and wisdom that comes from perseverance.

My graduation ceremony concluded at 12:15 pm—over so soon for such a tremendous moment in my life, and the lives of my peers. We graduates then gathered outside the cathedral, hugging and congratulating each other, ready for that iconic moment. As one, we all tossed our mortarboards in the air in celebration. I almost felt like I was in a movie, that glorious moment when beaming students flung the symbols of their achievements sky-high. But this was truly happening for me. I was not playing pretend or acting a role. I was not an imposter, despite the countless times imposter syndrome had plagued me. I was authentic and I deserved to be there. And just like that, the event was over. Tired after my sleepless night, early start, and floods of emotions, it was time to head home.

Though the ceremony was over, the celebrations were not. The rest of my family were waiting for me, ready to share a feast that they had planned in my honour. The joy and laughter were integrated with stories and recollections of the journey that had brought us all to this moment - a shared success. The evening was spent in the company of loved ones, celebrating not just my achievement, but the collective effort and support that had made it possible. I looked around at the beautiful reminder of the love and encouragement that surrounded me, thankful for each and every person present and the smiles on their faces.

I owe a great deal of my success to the incredible teachers who have guided and supported me throughout my academic journey. Their dedication, patience, and encouragement have been invaluable tools for their students to thrive on. The teachers I have encountered on my course have been a constant source of inspiration. They challenged me to think critically, to push beyond my limits, and to believe in my abilities. I am deeply grateful for their unwavering support, and for the knowledge they have imparted. Their impact on my life extends far beyond the classroom, and I will carry their lessons with me, always. Throughout my academic journey, I have learned many valuable lessons that have shaped me into the person I am today. I understand the importance of perseverance, especially during those challenging times when giving up seemed like the easier option. I have discovered the power of collaboration, and the strength that comes from working with others towards a common goal. Most importantly, I have learned to embrace failure as a stepping stone to success, understanding that each setback is an opportunity for growth and improvement. I also recognise that these tools are pearls of wisdom to pass on, echoing the encouragement and growth I have been so lucky to experience. The secret to success should not be a secret at all, and I endeavour to share this.

As I embark on the next chapter of my academic journey, I am filled with excitement and anticipation for what lies ahead. The change of direction was unexpected, but working on my degree unlocked a new dream and an old passion. Starting my MA in Creative Writing is not just a continuation of my education, but a significant symbol of who I have become.

When once I was near terrified at the thought of higher education, that dread has been replaced with faith in myself and a hunger to learn. The program will enable me to refine my craft, explore new genres, and connect with like-minded individuals who share my passion for storytelling. I know that I will be faced once again with unforeseen hurdles, sleepless nights, and the gnaw of self-doubt, but I am now equipped to combat these, along with anything else that may stand in my path. I am eager to immerse myself in the world of creative writing, learn from experienced writers, and push the boundaries of my imagination. I now have a future brimming with endless possibilities, and the knowledge that I can climb to great heights, triumphing with tenacity. My graduation is not an end, but the start of a new chapter, the start of a new path, and hopefully the evolution of who I am. Who knows, maybe Yusra the published author is waiting for me behind the next door.

Conclusion

Triumphs of Tenacity by Yusra Mariyam is my testament to the power of resilience, determination, and the human spirit.

Starting a new life in the UK at only seven years old naturally set me at a disadvantage compared to my peers, leaving me to learn how to navigate a new country, master a second language, and find my place in a society so different from anything I had previously experienced. The hurdles I faced as I stepped into this new world and integrated myself into British society developed my spirit into one of robust determination, forming a child who could rise to meet challenges with resilience. I am proud of that child, looking back at how I steered my way so fearlessly through the unknown.

As life's challenges continued to throw me curveballs, seeing my career aspirations crumble for reasons beyond my control, and impossible to change, saw my life take a different route. I embraced my role as a mother and a homemaker wholeheartedly, and the many hardships and obstacles that came with this role continued to fuel my determination and resolve. However, I lost focus on myself.

Raising my children was by far one of the most challenging but fulfilling periods of my life, riddled with many moments where I needed to call upon the determination

I had mastered during childhood. However, by pouring all of my love and care into my children's growth and development, I forgot to keep in touch with that part of me that had always shown such determination in pursuing my own evolution.

It was only by sheer chance that the idea of adult education came my way, and though it was never something I had seen for my future, I inexplicably took the leap, surprising even myself. The realisation that opportunities, no matter how unexpected, should be seized with full enthusiasm was something that changed the trajectory of my life, shining a light on a new path for me to tread.

Overcoming the self-doubt and anxiety that came with this sudden change in my journey turned out to be harder than the course itself. I had to dig deep and reclaim that part of me that had once been so understanding of the need for personal evolution, to reconnect with my inner child and the boldness that had fuelled me during that huge shift to life in the UK.

As my university course progressed, I drew on the wisdom that my late abba had imparted to me throughout my life, understanding his words with a new perspective and using them to drive me on. My husband, siblings, and children supported me, offering encouragement and tutoring. I learned how to embrace the insights of three generations, how to ask for help, and how to fall back on others with trust when I needed them. This was not my only realisation.

I became aware of the importance of conquering fears and focusing on vanquishing hurdles, rather than fleeing from them. I left university not only with a degree in International Business but with a fresh outlook on life altogether—skills that will hold equal value in the next chapters of my life.

I also rediscovered old passions that had long been forgotten during the trials, tribulations and sheer love that had come along with motherhood. The 'Legal Aspects of Business' module saw the keen interest my teenage self had once had in a career in law, whilst the written assignments brought back my love of writing. Reconnecting with these old dreams came with the understanding that even when a door seems to have closed, it might not actually be locked. Pursuing new goals, as well as revisiting old ones, revealed how broad my horizons could be, and the many possible paths that I could take. Thanks to my abba's teachings, and the determination that I had honed during my course, I now understand that though the paths may be turbulent, whichever one I choose can be met with a resilience that will guide me through to the light that is certainly waiting for me at the other end.

Though my venture into higher education has changed me profoundly, I am still the same person as I was before, walking through the same life. Keeping in touch with my heritage and culture whilst integrating with professional norms has been an important part of my experience. My beliefs and background do not have to be compromised for the sake of fitting in. Embracing diversity and understanding others whilst holding onto our roots is an essential part of life. We do not become 'new' people, there is no 'old' me, we simply become improved versions of ourselves, armed with the ability to weather the storms.

Embarking on my next adventure, an MA in creative writing, has shown me the flexible and meandering nature of life. Though some things seem to be outlined by fate, the choices we make along the way are within our control. Embracing the unexpected, and using our past as a lesson, propels us into the next chapter of our walk through life. The transformative nature of education, combined with the power of determination, transform the obstacles that stand in our way into paving stones along the path to success.

We can inspire ourselves as much as we draw inspiration from others. My hope is that anyone who has followed my journey can also follow in my footsteps. Like me, you can reclaim resilience, tenacity, and passion, even in the face of the most formidable challenges, conquering the impossible by defying all odds.

About The Author

Yusra Mariyam is an inspiring example of the strength of the human spirit, proving the power of perseverance and determination. Born in Bangladesh and raised in the UK from the age of seven, she faced the myriads of challenges that came with integrating into a new society. Yet, despite her young age, she conquered them all. Her life has been one of overcoming adversity and defying the odds that were stacked against her from an early age.

After leaving school without the qualifications she needed to pursue her dreams, her focus changed from a career path to motherhood. She raised her six children with determination not to let academic difficulties hold them back, as they had for her.

When by chance her time finally came, Yusra endeavoured to complete a course in International Business Studies at Anglia Ruskin University. Despite the challenges she faced on her journey through education as a mature student, she harnessed the resilience she had honed during her early years and used it to thrive.

In 2024, Yusra graduated with First-Class Honours, proving to all that courage and determination can lead to self-empowerment and success. Her ability to reclaim her inner strength and rise above numerous setbacks—both personal and academic— has made her a symbol of triumph, even when faced with seemingly impossible hurdles. Her story serves as a guide for those facing their own struggles, standing as proof that adversity, when met with resilience, can only make us stronger.

Through her memoir, *Triumphs of Tenacity*, Yusra inspires others to see past their battles and embrace the personal evolution that waits on the other side. With a passion for the transformative nature of education, and understanding the lessons that come with adversity, Yusra stands as a testament to the belief that it is never too late to achieve greatness. She continues to advocate for lifelong learning, empowerment, and the importance of self-belief.

Printed in Dunstable, United Kingdom